The Skill in Means

(Upāyakauśalya)

Sūtra

The Skill in Means

(Upāyakauśalya)

Sūtra

Translated by

MARK TATZ

MOTILAL BANARSIDASS PUBLISHERS
PRIVATE LIMITED • DELHI

First Edition: Delhi, 1994
Reprint Edition: Delhi, 2001

ISBN: 81-208-0915-7

Also available at:
MOTILAL BANARSIDASS
41 U.A. Bungalow Road, Jawahar Nagar, Delhi 110 007
8 Mahalaxmi Chamber, Warden Road, Mumbai 400 026
120 Royapettah High Road, Mylapore, Chennai 600 004
236, 9th Main III Block, Jayanagar, Bangalore 560 011
Sanas Plaza, 1302 Baji Rao Road, Pune 411 002
8 Camac Street, Kolkata 700 017
Ashok Rajpath, Patna 800 004
Chowk, Varanasi 221 001

Printed in India
BY JAINENDRA PRAKASH JAIN AT SHRI JAINENDRA PRESS,
A-45 NARAINA, PHASE-I, NEW DELHI 110 028 AND
PUBLISHED BY NARENDRA PRAKASH JAIN FOR
MOTILAL BANARSIDASS PUBLISHERS PRIVATE LIMITED,
BUNGALOW ROAD, DELHI 110 007

To my gurus
Kalu Rinpoche and Dezhung Rinpoche

Contents

INTRODUCTION

The *Skill in Means* is a sūtra of the early Mahāyāna school. Its composition may date from the first century B.C.

Along with the Original Buddhist sūtras, the *Skill in Means* is interlocutory in format. Its setting is the Jeta Grove at Śrāvastī, among a community of monks and Bodhisattvas (section 1). At the conclusion, however, the audience is described as the four assemblies (male and female monastics, and male and female householders) plus gods and other supernatural beings (sections 175, 178). In any case, the chief protagonists of the scripture fall into two camps: elders of the monastic community, and Bodhisattvas.

In response to the question posed by a Bodhisattva named Jñānottara ("one rich in knowledge"), the Buddha gives a discourse that accomplishes two aims: (1) the introduction of "skill in means" into the fabric of buddhist ethical life, and (2) dispelling misinterpretations of the nature of the historical Buddha, especially in regard to certain events that befell him. The address of these two issues forms two distinct sections of the work. The second of these is introduced as a formal account of doctrine (*dharma-paryāya*) known as "skill in means" (section 71). Yet the two parts do not appear to have been separately composed and then stitched into a text. The life of the Buddha (Parts Two and Three) and the ethics of Bodhisattvas (Part One) are the warp and the woof; they are woven into a sūtra by the concept of skill in means. Later accounts of Mahāyāna doctrine incorporate this material into sections entitled "skill in means" and "the life-span of the Tathāgata (Thus-Come-One)"; consequent neglect of the *Skill in Means* may have saved it from all but the minor glosses and alterations of its redaction in the Ratnakūṭa collection.

"Skill in means" is presented, in the opening discourse of the Buddha, as practice of the six perfections with a mental focus upon the attainment of Buddhahood. To that end, a key component of any practice is the dedication of merit earned by the deed to the immediate welfare and ultimate awakening of others. Skilful giving (*dāna*) is adduced as an example. Dedication of the merit derived from generosity gives rise to rewards that are wonderful beyond all reasonable expectations, because "gifts become great when given with great thoughts"(12).

Among the personae of the sūtra, Bodhisattvas are chiefly represented—after the Buddha himself—by Jñānottara. Two others, named *Gaṇapramukharāja and Priyaṁkara, interact with women in ways that illustrate skill in means (23ff, 48ff). The elders who observe this with shock are represented chiefly by Ānanda; others include Maudgalyāyana, whose famed magical powers fail in the face of the Buddha's skill in means, and Kāśyapa, who is quickest to adopt the Bodhisattva paradigm. Not all members of the assembly are converted by the dramatic events and recitals: those who are not "fit vessels" do not even see or hear them (176).

In its approach to the life of Śākyamuni, the sūtra attempts to resolve an issue that has caused discord among the schools. Certain events of his career seem to denote a mixed inheritance of *karma*. The Buddha failed to obtain alms-food on one occasion, and on another his foot was pierced by a thorn. These and other problematic incidents are listed in such texts as the *Vinaya* of the Mūlasarvāstivāda school and the *Therāpadāna* of the Theravāda, each being explained as the residue of a past misdeed. That scholiastic explanation seems to have been unacceptable to the masses of Buddhists of an age that virtually deified the founder in literature and art. The sūtra makes a definitive response: those untoward events represent displays of karmic recompense contrived by the Buddha for the edification of others; they are instances of his skill in means. The same explanation applies to deeds he performed in the past, as a Bodhisattva, that appear to have given rise to that recompense. As the brahman youth Jyotipāla, for example, he refused to pay respect to the Buddha Kāśyapa, instead saying sarcastically, "Where is the awakening in a shaven head?" This has been considered by scholars as the cause of severe austerities that he underwent, during his last lifetime, for six years prior to the great awakening. In actuality, Jyotipāla behaved in that disrespectful way as part of a trick to convert five brahman companions who are unknown to the earlier accounts.

To thus purify the Buddha of all apparent imperfection does not of itself make the text "greater vehicle". But its corollary, the doctrine of skill in means, becomes a guiding principle in the ethics of Bodhisattvas, or at least in those of high-stage Bodhisattvas (the *Mahāsattvas*). Skill in means as a moral principle is established, in the important first part of the sūtra, by a discourse on the perfections; it is then illustrated by past-life tales and by contemporaneous events. Ethics for the Bodhisattva, to put the matter briefly, is based upon the code for all monastics (the Vinaya), yet it is not circumscribed by it. Skill in means may supersede the monastic rule. The Buddha illustrates this supersession with the most shocking examples he can discover in his own past lives. Not only did he commit murder—he also broke celibacy.

Insofar as we can ascertain the historical development of Mahāyāna Buddhism, texts dealing with philosophy (*prajñā*) emerge slightly earlier than those dealing with ethics. The philosophic sūtras have been studied as they are extant in the *Perfection of Wisdom*, the *Kāśyapa Chapter*, and other early scripture; they seek to recapture the mystic intuition of original Buddhism, as the new "wisdom" school sees it, from the scholastic analytics of the Abhidharma schools. The importance of philosophy is not to be diminished. Discourses upon the emptiness of all phenomena (which are found in the *Skill in Means* scripture as well) do not compare with developments in ethics, however, in making the new movement conspicuous. The picture of monks playing fast and loose in their relations with women is an integral part of the greater-vehicle paradigm to this day, as the other schools see it.

The concepts of perfect wisdom and skill in means are complementary and nearly co-arising in the early Mahāyāna; in later literature the tension between them drives the Bodhisattva career. So wisdom is the sixth perfection, while skill in means subsumes the initial five. From wisdom flows a technical vocabulary that has been explored by Conze, Lamotte and others. From skill in means derives a corresponding set of terms for the functions (the "bodies") of a Buddha, for "pure lands", and for the Bodhisattva stages.

Buddhists in India were distinguished as a community of religieux by adherence to the word of the Buddha as codified in sūtra and in vinaya. The *Skill in Means* shows very clearly a function of early Mahāyāna sūtras: to state principles in forceful and dogmatic terms, so as to rally the Buddhist community from a crisis of values, a crisis exemplified by arguments over the nature of the Buddha. They do not in fact succeed in converting the community as a whole. Rather, adherents to the Greater Vehicle come to constitute a vigorous minority.

In religious affairs, however, no one paradigm need absolutely obtain universal acceptance. Schism is a practical alternative. Whether or not the Buddhist householder in India felt sectarianism to constitute a crisis in itself, the persistence of differences did not inhibit cooperation and spiritual accomplishment by individuals.

1. Time, Place and Person

The setting of the sūtra is the Jeta Grove, which puts it in a class with the *Mahāvastu* and the *Lalitavistara*.[1] By contrast, the *Kāśyapaparivarta*, the *PWA*, and *PWP* take place at Vulture Peak. The *PW Vajracchedikā* is set in the Jeta Grove, and its opening passages strikingly resemble those of the *Upāya*, save that in the *PWV* the key to boundless merit through giving is non-reliance upon things, rather than dedication of the merit. According to Nakamura, both the Jeta Grove and Vulture Peak are settings for the earliest Mahāyāna sūtras (1976:70).

There may be a reference to Surāṣṭra (*Up* 32), but this comes in the context of a past-life tale.[2]

The size of a sūtra's audience tends to expand in later versions, making this a difficult guide to chronology. According to the Ratnakūṭa version of the *Upāya* (the Tibetan version), its assembly consists of 8,000 monks and 16,000 Bodhisattvas; this is identical to classical versions of the *Kp* (xi). The Fa-ch'eng version gives 84,000 monks and 16,000 Bodhisattvas. The Chinese translation of the Ratnakūṭa seems to number the Bodhisattvas at 12,000. The earliest scheme for Mahāyāna sūtras, according to Nakamura (1976:70), is 1,250 monks alone, as found in *PWA*. *PWV*Skt gives 1,250 monks and numerous Bodhisattvas. The longer versions of the Perfection of Wisdom sūtras give the same or a larger number of monks, and numerous Bodhisattvas; they add 500 nuns, laymen, and laywomen, thus fulfilling an earlier scheme of "four assemblies". *Mpps* discusses the various enumerations found in *PW* sūtras in terms of the profundity of the text as against the intellectual capacity of the audience (1:233-34). The *Upāli* (Chinese) gives 1,250 monks and numerous Bodhisattvas; the Tibetan gives 500 as the number of monks.

Nakamura apparently errs in describing the assembly of *Kp* as 1,250 monks alone in the earlier (second century) translation by Lokakṣema: it is 1,250 monks and 12,000 Bodhisattvas (xi). That leaves only *PWA* with an assembly defined simply as 1,250 monks. This is no ground, however, upon which to conclude that 1,250 monks is an "original assembly" for Mahāyāna sūtras.

More than one scholar has remarked that *PWA* is a continuation, in one sense at least, of "auditor" (*śrāvaka*) concerns. The theme of the *Aṣṭa* is wisdom extended to attainment of Buddhahood; there is little in it of the ethical theme of helping others, as *PWP* provides at length. This holds true for the *Aṣṭa*, and for *Rg* up to its final chapters (29-32), which have no counterpart in the *Aṣṭa*; it may explain why the *Aṣṭa* addresses itself exclusively to monks who are arhats. To infer, however, that skill in means linked to concern for others is a late enlargement of the Bodhisattva ideal,[3] or that dedication of merit when it appears in the *Aṣṭa* is a late stratum of the text,[4] is not warranted, for to do so is to ignore the first principle of Buddhist hermeneutics: a teaching is directed in all cases to listeners at a particular stage of spiritual development.[5] Further, wisdom in the *Rg* is one among the set of perfections (*Rg* 1:5, 25, etc). I will attempt to show that redactors of *PWA* have isolated the teachings on wisdom from those on ethics for separate presentation, and redactors of *PWP* and other later sūtras have re-combined them.

2. Ānanda

The *Aṣṭa* begins (tr. Conze 83):

> Thus have I heard at one time. The Lord dwelt at Rājagṛha, on the Vulture Peak, together with a great gathering of monks, with 1,250 monks, all of them Arhats . . . with the exception of one single person, i.e. the Venerable Ānanda.

Ānanda appears twice in this passage. He is the speaker who has "heard", and in this role he represents the Buddhist community; he reappears at the close of the discourse to formally acknowledge and receive the teaching.[6] He does the same in the *Upāya*, and this role needs no further examination for the present.

Why is Ānanda to be singled out for denigration in this passage? He is traditionally subjected to this criticism: all vinaya accounts save that of the Mahīśāsaka relate, in detail, the criticism made of him after the passing of the Buddha.[7] That Ānanda is no arhat is no special concern, however, of Mahāyāna sūtras. In the *Aṣṭa* it is Śāriputra who plays the role of convert to the new wisdom; Ānanda is confined to the perfunctory role of witness, asking questions such as "Why does the Lord smile at this?" Here in the *Upāya* it is Ānanda who needs correction. To determine why he is the central antagonist in *Up* is to move directly to the central concern of the sūtra.

The concern of the *Upāya* is not simply ethical. The *Question of Upāli* makes many of the same points of ethics as Part One of this *Question of Jñānottara*: the ethic of the Bodhisattva surpasses the ethic of abstention, sensuality is less grave an offense than aversion, and a Bodhisattva who commits a transgression does not lose his status as Bodhisattva so long as he retains the intention of reaching awakening (*Upāli* 39-42). In the *Upāli*, however, ethics is revised in light of the new wisdom and the "straw man" is Śāriputra, whereas in the *Jñānottara* the context of ethics is skill in means.

Ānanda attempts to enforce monastic discipline, and celibacy in particular, upon Bodhisattvas. He spies a Bodhisattva in apparent intimacy with a woman, and takes it as his duty to report it to the Buddha (*Up* 23-29). He is proven wrong by the Bodhisattva's ability to levitate; the lesson teaches him not to question the skill in means of a Bodhisattva (25). Following a second incident in which a Bodhisattva flirts with impropriety, the lesson of skill in means is again addressed to Ānanda (50, 57). Then near the end of Part One, Ānanda testifies to his conversion (58-59): the Bodhisattva's "thought of omniscience" transcends states of mind; it is a panacea.

Ānanda appears as the Buddha's attendant in the "life of the Buddha" sections; this is closer to his traditional role as bystander. "What deed did the Buddha perform of which this thorn is the recompense," he asks, and the Buddha delivers, to an audience that needs it, a teaching on *karma* and its recompense (143). The point of the incident is that the thorn that sticks in his foot is but an instance of his skill in means, whereas the Buddha himself is no longer subject to the effects of his past deeds. Later, Ānanda pities his master for eating horse-feed for three months, and is taught better (161). At a place where older accounts show Ānanda to shine—he replaces the Buddha in delivering a discourse—the *Upāya* replaces him with Kāśyapa (164).

Ānanda is not known to tradition as having been equipped with monkish misogyny or with zeal to supervise monastic discipline. In the early literature he is continually faulted for liking women. Were this the crux of the issue, the Buddha's half-brother Nanda would make a more apt antagonist.[8]

In my opinion, Ānanda must have been a target of generalized resentment even during the lifetime of the Buddha, whom he served as personal attendant (*upasthāyaka*). See this friendly portrait of him:

> As a matter of fact, Ānanda was very popular among all lay disciples of the Buddha. As he was the closest associate of the Buddha, some expected to gain the Buddha's favor through him. . . People who wanted to see the Buddha, first went to Ānanda.

But this picture seethes with potential for loss of reputation. For some thirty years, Ānanda was the one to tell visitors and disciples, "I'm sorry, the Teacher cannot see you just now."

In the *Upāya*, Ānanda displays the fault of underestimating the Buddha, a fault that may stem from intimacy with him. When he informs upon the Bodhisattva whom he spied sitting together with a woman, he prefaces his disclosure with a remark bearing upon the Buddha's purported omniscience that might be described as sneering (23). The sense of it is, "Why need I tell the 'all-knowing one' of this?" After his conversion, he acknowledges the superiority of the Bodhisattva's aspiration, designated throughout this text (and in the *Upāli* as well) as an aspiration for omniscience (*sarvajñacitta = bodhicitta*). He testifies that Bodhisattvas resemble Mount Sumeru: the turquoise, etc. sides of the great mountain color the sky on each side blue, etc. So a person's thinking—whether angry, passionate or devoted—is colored by the thought of omniscience however she may stand before a Bodhisattva.

The term "knowing all" (*sarvajña*) may not be meant by Mahāyānists to imply that the Buddha knows everything. By analogy, the Sarvāstivāda school takes its name from its assertion that the past and the future exist; it does not literally assert "the existence of everything". According to the account of Vasumitra, the Lokottaravādins assert that the Buddha knows all *dharmas* instantaneously (20). This may be understood, in line with later Sautrāntika-Yogācāra theories of perception, as an assertion of *yogipratyakṣa*: What he knows he knows directly, by mental cognition. In the early centuries B.C., the doctrine of his omniscience may have been no more than necessary postulate to *jātaka* and *avadāna* literature: the Buddha remembers his own and others' past lives.[9]

Ānanda doubts the Buddha's freedom from *karma* (*Up* 143), an error he also makes in the *Vimalakīrti*.[10]

Such obtuseness is Ānanda's most heinous crime in the earlier literature as well, for it leads him to neglect to request the Buddha to remain alive until the end of the age. In some versions of that incident, he is specifically accused by the Buddha of defective understanding.[11] He may have seemed more criminal than ever to Buddhists of later times who attributed grand capabilities of the Buddha but had to live without his presence.

Ānanda takes for granted not only the Buddha, but the teachings as well, according to the earlier accounts. Although he retains all the scriptures in memory, he has not put them into practice and thereby attained arhatship. To followers of the Mahāyāna, Ānanda may represent those elders who cling to the sūtras contained in their own canon and refuse to acknowledge that there are others. Section 11 of the *Upāya* states that a Bodhisattva who is dull may acquire merit surpassing that of any savant—and the Ratnakūṭa version adds, "including Ānanda".[12]

Ānanda is cast as a doubter in the *Mahāvastu* as well. The teaching of ten Bodhisattva stages is addressed to him, because he quibbles, "If a *bhūmi* is immeasurable, how can more than one be adduced?" (*Mv* 1:78). And at 3:47-56, he underestimates Kāśyapa.

3. The Upāyakauśalya *as a Life of the Buddha*

Parts Two and Three of the *Upāya* presuppose a biographical account of the Buddha's life, but their treatment of its events and of its issues renders the biographical approach irrelevant. The sūtra thus links the *Mahāvastu* with developments in Buddhology found in the *Lotus*, the *Vimalakīrti*, and other great Mahāyāna sūtras.

A close reading suggests that the *Upāya* falls between the *Mahāvastu* and the *Lalitavistāra* as a biography of the Buddha. The *Mv* (in some of its versions) is known to the composer of the *Upāya*, and the *Mv* is likewise known to the composer of the *Lv*. The later, Ratnakūṭa recension of *Up* knows *Lv*, but it cannot be said that *Lv* knows *Up*.

Like the *Mv*, the *Upāya* relates incidents of the Buddha's final lifetime to occurrences in the distant past. An important proviso is attached, however, to this method. The *Upāya* follows that approach, a traditional method of explication by past-life tales, in order to criticize it: the deeds of the Buddha are not dependent upon *karma*, as are the deeds of unawakened beings—they depend upon the needs of the present and are inspired by skill in means. The *Upāya* is fundamentally anti-biographical, insofar as a Buddha is concerned.

Details of treatment and phrasing that relate *Up* to *Mv* and to *Lv* are presented in the annotation to Part Two of the translation below.[13] The list of "karmic connections" in Part Three is not identical to that of any other known account, but strongly resembles that of *Msv* in some details. The past-life tales are drawn from literary sources or constructed from common motifs. One such motif concerns 500 merchants on a trading venture: in a tale of the *Mv*, the Bodhisattva kills himself to save them from disaster; in the *Up* he slays a suspected robber (132-37).

The *Mv* was founded as a text in the second century B.C.[14] The *Upāya* should therefore be placed in the first century B.C., a date conforming to its relationship with *PW* literature.

There is no biography as such in the early strata of Buddhist literature, although *sūtra* constitutes an anecdotal, non-chronological account of Śākyamuni's quest for liberation and his subsequent teaching career, and *vinaya* constitutes an account of the building of the monastic order.[15] There is no full biography even by the time of the *Upāya*. The *Mv* concludes with the conversion of the brothers Kāśyapa, and the *Lv* with the first formal teaching. The *Mahāvadāna* (Pali *Mahāpadāna*) sūtra recounts the final life of the past Buddha Vipaśyin up to his founding of the order. This text is thought to derive from the period following King Aśoka.[16] We may infer from it the existence of a genre of exemplary biography (or hagiography) focusing upon renunciation, search and salvation, and including narratives of a Buddha's birth, development and teaching career; such texts developed, in literary form, from the artwork and popular lore that surrounded pilgrimage sites from the time of Aśoka. The biographies agree on motifs such as the descent from Tuṣita heaven and birth from his mother's side. For example, a sūtra passage on life in the palace, "I was delicate, O monks. . ." evolves into the elaborate description found in the *Mv*.[17]

A narrative of the Buddha's last days, culminating in the council held at Rājagṛha after his passing, is attached to some versions of Vinaya as an ecclesiastical history of the transmission of leadership.[18] This old Skandhaka narrative is not the model for later biographies.[19] The *Upāya* is not concerned with it and pays the parinirvāṇa no attention at all.[20]

For the most part, the *Upāya* addresses incidents belonging to the common tradition that are of special concern because they seem to contradict the transcendentalist conception of Śākyamuni. Most notably, it offers interpretations of the early, pleasure-filled life at home and of the ten events of his teaching career that seem to result from bad *karma*. Questions such as "Why does the Bodhisattva take a wife?" (*Up* 91) follow a format found in the *Mv* and continued in the *Lv*; they adduce objections to the transcendentalist view.

Although it is not a formal biography, the *Upāya* is treated by tradition as a Mahāyāna "life of the Buddha". The Tibetan historian Bu-ston (A.D. 1290-1364) presents the life of Śākyamuni from *Lv* and *Msv* and refers to the *Upāya* for the esoteric meaning of events (*History* 789:3-4, tr. 2:72). After the *Upāya* has accomplished its fusion of transcendentalism with skill in means, biography as such recedes in importance. Buddhology then becomes a study of "three bodies (*tri-kāya*)" theory, and the only question posed by ultramundanism is how soon a Bodhisattva attains the powers of a Buddha.

4. Ultramundanism and Skill in Means

A monograph on the subject by Michael Pye (1978) traces the use of the terms *upāya* and *upāya-kauśalya*. Being limited to previously translated works, that study misses the *Upāyakauśalya* sūtra, and consequently encounters difficulty in considering the data of the *Mv*. Of the *Mv* it observes, "The concept of skilful means [sic] is not associated here. . .with the supra-historical view of Buddhahood" (69). On the other hand, it notes astutely, further on, that "it is perhaps indicative of a general continuity in Buddhist thought that the one reference to *upāyakauśalya* (skill in means) in the *Mahāvastu* is to be found in the section on 'apparitions' in the account of the tenth *bhūmi*". (81n.)[21]

That phrase of the *Mv* is indeed translated by Jones as "skilful in his expedients", but the Sanskrit is *svavidhāna-kovida* (1:178:1), literally "skilled in his own methodology"; it is followed in the next verse by the common epithet *vāda-siṁha*, "lion among teachers". The concept of skill in means may be implicit here, in association with the Buddha's ability to teach through "presentations" (*upahāra*), but the absence of the term *upāya-kauśalya* in the *Mv* leads one to believe that it had no currency at the time.

The Buddha is described as "skilled in means" (*upāya-kusala*) in a verse of the Pali canon (*Theragāthā* 158). In a stanza of the *Suttanipāta* (321) a teacher of doctrine, like a good boatman, is a "skilful knower of means" (*upāyaññu-kusalo*, cited Pye 1978:120). No other usage in Pali is demonstrably older than the *Up*. The Jātakas apply "skill in means" to the Buddha when he converts Nanda from passion to religion;[22] at other places it is associated with *paññā*, "wisdom" (*ibid.* 120-21 and n.). In general, *upāya* in the Pali canon has its ordinary sense of "means", as applied to the path; *kusala* has its ordinary sense of "skill", as applied to effective practice of the path.[23]

"Skill in means" is not a primary term of early Buddhism; its earliest technical application is to Buddhology, with secondary application to scriptural exegesis. The *Mv* stops short of deriving the concept from transcendentalist Buddhology, which is why the *Mv* is not Mahāyāna.

In the *Upāya*, "skilled in means" is a quality of Śākyamuni, and of Bodhisattvas in general. The life of Śākyamuni is traditionally divided, by the great awakening, into Bodhisattvahood and Buddhahood. The *Upāya* blurs this distinction with a series of assertions regarding the Bodhisattva: he could have attained Buddhahood in many of his past lives, his state of peaceful concentration is equivalent to the auditor's nirvāṇa, and he could have taught doctrine without leaving Tuṣita heaven (72-75). Furthermore, he does not in fact leave Tuṣita, but performs the deeds of a Bodhisattva who is living his final life by means of magical creations (*nirmita*, 76). In the *Mv*, the creation of phantom bodies is a quality proper to Buddhas.[24] To assign it to a Bodhisattva makes the *Upāya* a work of the Mahāyāna.

The earlier schools to some extent view the Bodhisattva as transcendental. The Bodhisattva is not impelled to his last rebirth by sense-desire, nor does he develop in embryo as does an ordinary being (Rockhill 1884: 188, Vasumitra 21). The line between Bodhisattva and Buddha is still clearly drawn, however, even in the *Mv*: the Bodhisattva in Tuṣita heaven has overcome the hindrances (*nīvaraṇāni viṣkambhitāni*) without yet obtaining the sovereignty of doctrine (*aprāpte dharmarājye*; *Mv* 1:147:15-148:1).

To all Buddhists, the Buddha is by definition ultramundane in some sense. A point at issue among them in the pre-Mahāyāna period is whether he has completely transcended the effects of past deeds. Some works explain the thorn piercing his foot as the residue (*avaśeṣa*) of *karma* from killing a man with a spear (*Apadāna, Msv*). Such reasoning is not acceptable to the Transcendentalists, who regard transcendence of karmic causation to be a necessary quality of Buddhahood (Rockhill 1884:187, Vasumitra 18-21). To them the Buddha is not the ordinary person he appears to be, and the *Mv* in a famous paean describes his ordinary actions as instances of "conformity with the world" (*lokānuvartana*; *Mv* 1:163-70).

Corollary to this transcendentalist view is the view of all Buddhas as equivalent. Their careers become the expression of a universal pattern, and there is little to distinguish the *Mv* account of the last life of Dīpaṁkara, in Volume One, from that of Śākyamuni in Volume Two. And we read sentences such as (Vasumitra 21): "All the Bodhisattvas assume the forms of white elephants when they enter their mothers' wombs."[25]

The Lokottaravādins seem to have advanced divergent propositions in explaining some of the acts of the Buddha. They say, for example: (1) the Buddhas do not really teach in words, and (2) words can be uttered while in a state of *samādhi* (Rockhill 1884:187-88, Vasumitra 20, 23). The problem addressed in this case is, "How can the Teacher engage in teaching while withdrawn from sense data?" In the Mahāyāna, this question becomes a paradox of wisdom versus skill in means: the Bodhisattva knows that phenomena are "empty, signless and wishless", yet he acts so as to save sentient beings; he abides in peaceful *samādhi*—the absence of sense data—while functioning in the realm of sense-desire (*Up* 60).

The term *samādhi* ("concentration") does not appear in the *Mv* in that sense,[26] but *Lv* descibes the Bodhisattva as abiding in a state of concentration called *mahāvyūha* while he is in the womb (46:22, 47:2). In the *Upāya* he abides in *samādhi* in Tuṣita heaven and sends a magical creation into the womb. In the *Śūraṁgama-samādhi* sūtra, the *samādhi* called *śūraṁgama* enables the Bodhisattva to enjoy a home life among women while preaching the doctrine in other worlds as a Buddha.[27] A chapter of the *Lotus* entitled "The Life-span of the Thus Come One" establishes the proposition that birth into the Śākya clan is a device (*upāya*); in reality, he has been a full Buddha for many eons.[28] The *jātaka* conception dissolves in light of this approach, as does the last significant distinction among Śākyamuni, Dīpaṁkara, and other Buddhas of the past—a development prefigured in the *Upāya* when it says, "the Buddhas have the same element of *dharma*" (10).

5. Skill in Means and Perfection of Wisdom

The monk Kāśyapa, at *Upāya* 67, connects skill in means with the perfection of wisdom as complementary fields of Bodhisattva endeavor. The same equivalence is made in the *Perfection of Wisdom* and other sūtras.[29] At *Upāya* 106-7, on the other hand, an instance of skill in means is described as (R) "the outcome of the perfection of wisdom" or (Fa) "the outcome of perfection-of-wisdom gnosis". This passage of the sūtra, together with the occurrence in its self-title of the phrase "perfection of skill in means" (*Up* 177), would seem to indicate that the set of six perfections, including the perfection of wisdom, logically precedes the perfection of skill in means.

A hitherto perplexing section of the *PW* literature is observed to form the starting-point of the *Upāya*. Part One of the *Upāya* constitutes an expansion of the closing chapters (29-31) of the *Ratnaguṇasaṁcaya-gāthā*. These chapters are not expanded in the eight thousand line version (the *Aṣṭa*), as is most of the *Rg*. They are replaced in the *Aṣṭa* by the late, "almost turgid devotionalism" (Conze) of a search for the perfection of wisdom by the Bodhisattva (Ever-weeping) Sadāpramudita.[30] The elaboration of these closing chapters of the *Rg* has been separated from the *Aṣṭa* at some time during its redaction, and made the basis of this "Perfection of Skill in Means" sūtra. The story of Sadāpramudita replaced it prior to the Lokakṣema translation of the *Aṣṭa*, in 179 A.D.[31]

When the *Rg* has completed its survey of wisdom, it turns to the other perfections, meditation through giving (29:1ff). The conclusion to its account of "giving" is dedication of the merit to awakening. This is crowned by understanding the deed in the manner of wisdom. Dedication is described as increasing the merit of a good deed exponentially, and furthermore as the act of a Bodhisattva who is "wise and skilled in means" (*Rg* 31:16a). At the beginning of the *Upāya*, the Bodhisattva Jñānottara asks, "What is this thing called skill in means?" In answer, generosity is linked to dedication of merit, which causes the merit of giving to grow exponentially (*Up* 7). Thereupon, one fulfills the other perfections by giving "with skill in means" and understanding the deed in the manner of wisdom (18).

The *Rg* dates from as early as 100 B.C. (Conze, *PWA*, p. x).

In the story of Sadāpramudita that in *PWA* is substituted for the "skill in means" section of *Rg*, there appears an unnamed merchant's daughter (with five hundred maidservants) who bears a strong resemblance to Dakṣiṇottara of the *Upāya* (cp. *PWA* 283-90, *Up* 48-53). Each girl finds a Bodhisattva on her doorstep, falls in love with him, and is prevailed upon (in *Up*, "with skill in means") to generate an aspiration for awakening and then approach the Buddha.[32]

The chapter of *PWA* devoted to skill in means elucidates the concept with the simile of a master of archery who protects his companions from robbers in a forest (ch. 20, tr. 223-24, expanding *Rg* 20:2-4); the *Upāya* draws the same comparison in defending apparent licentiousness by a Bodhisattva (46-47). Other similes of that chapter of the *Rg* that have no counterpart in *PWA* and thus seem "rather obscure" (Conze 1968a:133) are not accounted for in *Up* either; they may turn up in some other Mahāyāna sūtra.

The rest of the chapter that *PWA* devotes to skill in means subsumes, under that heading, everything done by the Bodhisattva for the sake of others. The Bodhisattva does not allow wisdom to take him to nirvāṇa (termed "reality-limit") before all the qualities ("*dharmas*") of a Buddha have been achieved. "For it is this skill in means which protects him. His thought of enlightenment consists in just that fact that he does not want to leave all beings behind." Thus "upheld by skill in means, he increases his pure *dharmas* more and more" (tr. Conze 225).

In a chapter devoted to the nature of the Buddha, *PWA* explains that the epithet *tathāgata* derives from his possession of omniscience, which stems in turn from perfection of wisdom." But "the physical personality or the Tathāgata. . .is the result of the skill in means of the perfection of wisdom." This statement is followed by an account of the three bodies (*idem* 105-6).

The term Dharma-body, which also appears in that section, may mark this as a later stratum of *PWA*. All the 'Dharma-body' passages. . .are missing in the early Chinese translations 'except for the rather literal idea of "collection of the sūtras of the Buddha' " (*idem* xxi, n. 33, citing Lancaster). "Dharma-body" does not appear in the *Upāya*, save at one point of the Ratnakūṭa version: the Thus Come One does not really develop a backache, because "the. . .Buddhas are Dharma-bodies, they do not have gross bodies composed of the elements" (166; the last phrase comes from *Mv*). An apparently older notion, common to both versions of the *Upāya*, is his "indestructible, adamantine body" (*dhṛdha-vajrakāya*) that cannot be pierced by a thorn unless he should acquisce to it with skill in means (138). The Buddha who is born into the Śākya clan is only a magical creation (*nirmita*); he himself remains in Tuṣita heaven (76, but remains in what "body" is not specified). The body of birth bears the marks of a superman (14, R only; 160). In any case, "Dharma-body" in the classical conception is less likely to derive from a conception of the Buddha as "corpus of doctrine" than from his plenitude of good qualities, *dharmas*—a formulation common to *Up* and *PWA*.

We have seen that skill in means is linked to dedication of merit at the beginning of the *Upāya*, and in the *Rg* source-verses. The Bodhisattva completes every good deed with (1) an aspiration for Buddhahood and (2) dedication of the merit created by the deed to the achievement of Buddhahood by all sentient beings.

Dedication of merit is no "transference" of anything to someone else, but a means by which the Bodhisattva renews a commitment to goals that are long-range. Ordinary giving creates a short-term benefit for the recipient—giving food to a beggar, for example—and a relatively short-term benefit for the donor, such as rebirth in heaven. The Bodhisattva who makes a gift renounces the short-term benefit and makes a wish instead that the merit count toward Buddhahood; this surpasses the benefits of ordinary giving. In addition, the dedication itself creates even greater merit (*Up* 7=*Rg* 31:15-17).

Conze maintains that dedication of merit develops as antidote to the attitude whereby "merit is hoarded as treasure in heaven which no one can take away" (1962:203). But dedication of merit poses no contradiction to *karma* theory unless one takes *karma* theory as a brand of determinism in which there is no scope for altruistic motivation. Dedication constitutes a rejection of the religion of higher rebirth that has tempted Buddhists of all ages. We know from inscriptions that dedication held sway at the beginning of the Christian era (Basham 1981:33).

6. Skill in Means in Later Literature

The monograph by Pye, *Skilful Means*, contains an excellent treatment of skill in means in the classical sūtras of the Mahāyāna, and one need do little more here than to complete the presentation of the thesis concerning the textual tradition.

To recapitulate: The *Rg* would seem to be, as Conze has concluded, the earliest extant text of what became the "perfection of wisdom" tradition. But there is no hard—e.g., linguistic—evidence to mark the first two chapters of it, dealing with perfection of wisdom, as earlier than the final chapters on skill in means, nor even to suppose that the *Rg* considers itself a Perfection of Wisdom text. During the first century B.C. the *Rg* was expanded into a sūtra; the *Aṣṭa* contains most of that commentatorial expansion (what Hikata calls the Ur-text), but the *Aṣṭa* does not comment upon all the verses of *Rg*. Among the passages of *Rg* ignored by *PWA*, Chapters 29-31 are elaborated in Part One of the *Upāya*. Other parts of the lost expansion may yet be discovered in other sūtras.[33] *PWA* was redacted around the practice of "perfect wisdom" for an audience of abhidharmists. The integrity of perfection of wisdom and skill in means as parts of the path is clearly present in it, but *Rg* 29-31 was elaborated in separate text, the *Upāya*.

Subsequently, the *Upāya* did not receive the degree of attention that was accorded *PWA*. That it is cited several times by Śāntideva, and edited for inclusion in the Ratnakūṭa collection, shows that it remained in circulation; but it did not become the basis for a textual tradition. Perhaps it came to seem too bold in its imagery for Mahāyānists of later times who had settled back into the monastic style of life. In the great sūtras of later centuries, skill in means came to be treated as a topic; it is the subject of the second chapters of the *Lotus* and the *Vimalakīrti* sūtras, for example.[34]

The full flowering of the doctrine of skill in means may be found in Chapter Two of the *Vimalakīrti* sūtra. There too sexuality is an issue, thought somewhat muted. The Bodhisattva Vimalakīrti frequents places that are forbidden to monks; he puts himself at the service of ordinary persons. Yet he does not make the final break with the monastic identity, for he keeps celibacy, out of skill in means leading a home life in appearance only. A similar ambiguity is found in the *Upāya*: In all but one of the cases in which Bodhisattva monks are suspected of breaking celibacy, the accused is technically innocent. The complaints only highlight the petulance of the accusers; the Bodhisattva himself is not afraid to appear to have committed an infraction, but he does not actually do so unless it is absolutely necessary, to ensure the welfare of someone else.

Among the sūtra's instances of skill in means, those permitting unchastity and murder become in later literature the most famous, being cited as illustrations of the extreme. The point of these episodes, however, is that the Bodhisattva is willing to sacrifice his own spiritual advancement and delay his obtainment of nirvāṇa. He does not stray down the path of "erotic yogis" for whom unchastity is kind of blessing. Those who maintain celibacy in the *Upāya* are able to prove it by displays of levitation. The older yogic lore that spiritual power is lost by seduction—a lore that is codified in vinaya—is not contradicted.[35]

The Bodhisattva who is entitled to commit murder or to break celibacy is described as *Mahāsattva*, "great hero". Some commentators take this to limit the permission for dubious deeds to Bodhisattvas of a high stage, those for whom "skill in means" is an advanced attainment. Nevertheless, the *Bodhisattva-bhūmi* does not use the term "great hero" in its discussion of such cases.[36] So I do not take it to be the intention of the *Upāya*, nor of Asaṅga, to limit access to sex and murder (in appropriate circumstances) to celestial Bodhisattvas. The higher ethic wrought by skill in means affects the whole of the Bodhisattva path.

In the *Lotus*, skill in means is primarily a tool of hermeneutics. In the Single Vehicle (*eka-yāna*) theory for which the *Lotus* is a *locus classicus*, it is proposed that auditors are given teachings that are not definitive but are *upāya*, "expedient devices" (tr. Hurvitz), because auditors cannot cope with Bodhisattva teachings. This sense of "skill in means" is derivative. Of "single vehicle" theory, there is only a trace in the *Upāya*—the analogy of the splendid city, promulgated by Kāśyapa (61-68), in which auditors accept Bodhisattva doctrines in part. By contrast, it is the crucial term of the "conjured city" parable of the *Lotus* (ch. 7). The use of skill in means to explain discrepancies among Buddhist doctrines may be taken as a later development—a Mahāyāna response to doubts expressed as to the validity of the early Mahāyāna sūtras.

7. Textual Sources and the Present Translation

The *Upāyakauśalya* sūtra survives in full in two Tibetan, and three Chinese translations. Eight passages are cited in Sanskrit by Śāntideva (eighth century) in the *Śiksaṣāmuccaya*, all from Part One of the sutra.[37]

CHINESE TRANSLATIONS

(1) **Jñānottarabodhisattva-paripṛcchā*. Translated by Dharmarakaṣa at Tun-huang; Western Chin, A.D. 285.[38] Korean 48 = Taisho 345, Nanjio 52. 2 fascicules.

(2) *Idem* translated by *Nandi of India; Eastern China, A.D. 420. Edited by Bodhiruci in A.D. 713 as part of the Ratnakūṭa collection. K 22:38 = T 310:38, Nj 23:38. 3 fasc. Corresponds to Tibetan no. 2 below. Rendered into English by Chang et al. 1983.

(3) *Idem* tr. *Dānapāla of Oḍḍiyāna; Northern Sung, A.D. 1005. K 1424= T 346, Nj 926. 4 fasc.

TIBETAN TRANSLATIONS

(1) *Upāyakauśalyanāma-mahāyānasūtra.* Translated from Chinese no.1 by Wou Fa-ch'eng (Tib 'Gos Chos-grub, Skt **Dharmasiddha*) at Tun-huang, ca 755-849 A.D. Translated posterior to compilation of the catalogue of Ldan-dkar, which is probably 800 A.D.[39] Tōhoku 261 = Otani 927. 2 fascicules = 600 lines (*śloka*). Translation of technical terminology does not follow *Mhv* as we have it.

(2) *Sarvabuddhamahārahasya-Upāyakauśalya-Jñānottara-Bodhisattva-paripṛcchā*, "a *mahāyānasūtra* constituting one chapter (*parivarta*) of the Ratnakūṭa collection." Translated in Central Tibet (independently of Tibetan no.1) by Dānaśīla of Kaśmīr and Karmavarman of India[40] in collaboration with Ye-shes-sde. Revised by Ye-shes-sde ca 815, prior to completion of the *Mahāvyutpatti.*[41] 4 fasc., 30 lines. Toh 82=O 760:38, Ldan-dkar 62 (4 fasc., 53 lines). Corresponds to Chinese no. 2 above, with minor differences of arrangement.

OTHER VERSIONS

(1) Untitled fragment, Pelliot 1:90:3. 12 folios. A summary, or lecture notes, from Part Two of Tibetan no. 2.

(2) *Upāyakauśalya-sūtra.* Lost translaton from Indic attested at Ldan-dkar no. 173. 1 fasc.=300 lines. Possibly identical to *Up* listed at Mhv 1345, but discarded after the production of Tibetan no. 1.

(3) Untitled fragment, Stein catalogue no. 233. One folio of 6 lines recto and verso. Different content, same cast of characters as *Up.*[42]

(4) *Mahā-Upāyakauśalyasūtra.* In Chinese and in Tibetan (translated from Chinese). Ldan-dkar 253. 7 fasc. Presumably corresponds to Otani 1022, K 402. A different sūtra composed on the same topic.

Among the two Tibetan versions, the briefer (Tib 1=Ch 1 above), referred to hereafter as the Fa (-ch'eng) version, is genuinely earlier than R (the Ratnakūṭa version; Tib 2=Ch 2); it is not an edition bowdlerized for Chinese literati. Fa is the edition cited in the *Śikṣāsamuccaya.* R displays systematic (i.e. commentatorial) expansion, inflation of numbers, and alteration of concepts and terminology to accord with later works. The presentation of both versions here will demonstrate the growth of the sūtra, a process well attested in similar texts.[43]

Titles given in the *Up* may be seen at the head and foot of the translaton. Designations are also found at Sections 71 and 177.

The present translation is based upon Fa (Tibetan no.1); it is printed in large format. Printed in small format are variations and additions found in R (Tibetan no. 2). Greater variations are printed in left-hand (Fa) and right-hand (R) columns. Variations that are probably errors are only noted; the few grammatical differences that are clearly errors are ignored. Sanskrit passages from the *Śikṣāsamuccaya* are added with references to the Vaidya edition.[44] All other Sanskrit equivalents are reconstructions.

The text of R was edited from three editions: (1) Sde-dge, the Tshal-pa print published by Karma Triyana Dharmacakra in New Delhi; Dkon-brtsegs Cha 30a1-70b7. (2) Snar-thang, the block print in possession of Tibet House, New Delhi; Cha 79a6-139b7. (3) Peking, published by Otani University; 'I 4b6-50b5.

Fa was edited from four editions: (1) Sde-dge *ibid.* Mdo Za 283b2-310a7. (2) Snar-thang *ibid.* Zha 60b4-104b7. (3) Peking *ibid.* Zhu 298b3-327a6. (4) Lhasa, the block print in possession of the Institute of Higher Tibetan Studies, Sarnath; Zha 60b4-84b7.

The present translator does not read Chinese, but has been able to consult Chinese no. 2 (the Ratnakūṭa version) in the form of an English version published by Chang *et al.* in 1983. That translation is uncontaminated by reference to any other version. Although its divisions are haphazard, the annotation misleading, and the interpretations characterized by wild guesses at the meaning, that translation is close and conscientious: all phrases are represented, if not correctly translated, and in most cases the original Indic can be determined, if only by consultation with Tibetan no. 2. (But many passages are omitted.)

Chinese no. 3 seems to be a further expansion; it has not been considered, for in any case the inclusion of a third level would be unacceptably cumbersome to read.

Part of the work of translation was done under sponsorship of the Shastri Indo-Canadian Institute. Some transcription and editing of texts was capably performed by Mr. Norbu Samphel of New Delhi. A draft translation of the Fa-ch'eng version was done by Ms. Sylvia Waite of Vancouver, B.C. as a class project.

For photocopies of the edited Tibetan texts (in transliteration), contact Dr. Tatz by e-mail in c/o the publisher. (Not available on disk.)

Notes

1. So *Mv* 1:4; at 1:34 the events are located at Vulture Peak. This may represent a late Mahāyānist intrusion, like the Bodhisattvas who appear in the assembly in one version of the *Avalokita* sūtra (*ibid.* 2:293, see the comments by Rawlinson 1977:13).

2. Surāṣṭra (the Tibetan is *legs 'byor*) is present-day Kathiawar and Gujarat, down the Indus to the southeast; it had connections with Bactria and (later) with the Scythians and was, according to Hsüan Tsang, a center of Mahāyāna culture (Lamotte 1958: 410, 416, 495, 597).

3. Rawlinson 1977:16

4. Lethcoe 1977:268, 278 n. 26.

5. Lethcoe approaches a statement of the principle at 1977:264: "One becomes a Tathāgata through winning enlightenment. Although Tathāgatahood is the goal, the *Aṣṭa*'s major emphasis is not in exploring ways fully enlightened Bodhisattvas help beings, but in describing how one can become a Tathāgata. Behind the *Aṣṭa*'s analysis of the Bodhisattva's career is the presupposition that the best person to save others is a perfected being, a fully enlightened Bodhisattva."

6. Twice in *PWA*, at 266-69 and 299-300.

7. Przyluski 1926-28; see also *EB* 1:532. On the other hand, Ānanda is regarded by some groups as their leader after Kāśyapa dies; e.g. in the Sanskrit "Suvarṇavarṇa-avadāna", Roy 1971. (There is no reason to regard this text as Mahāyāna, contrary to *ibid.* 58.) According to some scholars, e.g. Bareau 1963: 140, these accounts of criticism of Ānanda, attributed to Kāśyapa at the Council of Rājagṛha, point to a later schism between their followers. For other sources for Ānanda see *Mpps* 1:94 n.1.

8. Nanda is converted, by stern measures, from excessive devotion to his wife; see Aśvaghoṣa, *Saundarananda.* He later turns against women; for example, he shows reluctance to take his turn expounding doctrine to nuns (*Saṁyuktāgama* cited Pachow 1951:31).

9. For a fourth-century discussion of omniscience taken literally, see *Mpps* 1:146-61.

10. Lamotte 1976:80-84, *Mpps* 1:516.

11. Bareau 1963:2:1:188-90.

12. Ānanda is famed for erudition. References *Mpps* 1: 223; see also 3:1547.

13. See also the discussion of Transcendentalism that follows in this Introduction. My annotation to Parts Two and Three draws upon other traditions of biography as well, but generally limits itself to sources earlier than the classical version of *Lv.* Besides those sources, see also the *Lokānuvartanā* sūtra as studied by Harrison 1982, a source for the *Mv* (*ibid.* 227).

14. Edgerton 1953:1:5 n.13. Translation of Buddha-biographies into Chinese dates from the end of the second century A.D.; see Lamotte 1958:724.

15. See the comments by Nanamoli at 1972:ii.

16. Lamotte 1958:721-22, Reynolds 1976:43-44.

17. References at Thomas 1949:47. For the view that the early biographies emphasize *karma* rather than miracles, see Granoff 1986.

18. Another purpose of the narrative may be to justify sectarian policies. See the comments on Ānanda, above; also Finot 1932, Frauwallner 1956, and qualifications by Lamotte at 1958:193-97, 722-23.

19. Lamotte 1958:196.

20. The *Mv*, however, describes itself as a Vinaya (1:2-3, discussed at translation 1:xii-xiii). On Chinese translations of other versions of *Mv* (or they may be other Mahāsaṁghika biographies), see Edgerton 1953:1:73n., Lamotte 1958:724, Warder 1980:34 n. 2.

21. I have had no opportunity to examine Tilak Kariyawasam, "The Development of Buddhology in the Early Mahāyāna and its Relation to the Pali Nikāyas", Ph.D. dissertation, Lancaster University, 1973 (reference Pye 1978:119n.) See the review of other literature by Pye 1978:1-2.

22. Cited *idem* 122n. from *Jātaka* no. 182; also Buddhaghoṣa, *Suttanipāta* commentary 2:274:20. But Aśvaghoṣa does not use the term in the *Saundarananda*.

23. Dictionary definitions of *upāya* are collected by Pye at 1978:11-12 and n. As "path" see e.g. *Visuddhimagga* 1:85, "means and way" (*upāyena pathena*); also *Vimuttimagga* fasc. 10, Samyutta 3:2:1. In a frequent usage in late sūtra (Aṅguttara 3:431 etc.) and commentatorial literature, "skill in means" subsumes "skill in gain [of wholesome states]" and "skill in [their] loss" (*āyakusalo, apāyakusalo*); see discusssion at Pye 1978:119-20.

24. *Mv* 1:177:13: *Paropahārāṁśca...upaharanti samyaksaṁbuddhāḥ sattvānām anugrahārtham;* also *Mv* 192:10-11: *ye tatra nirmitā bhikṣuḥ na caite bhikṣuṇo matā/ upahāram vadanti...* see also *ibid.* 181:12. On multiplication of bodies see *Mpps* 3:1352-53, *Bhadramāyā* 32, and tr. n. 115 below.

25. On the equivalency of Buddhas see Lamotte 1958:730-32, *EB* 3:360b-365b, Pye 1978:67-69.

26. "Concentration" appears in the *Mv* in an older usage, at 3:409:12 as *cetosamādhi*, from which one derives the power of invisibility.

27. Lamotte 1965:178, Pye 1978:54-55.

28. Hurvitz 1976:237-38. On the transcendentalist view of the Buddha see also Anesaki 1918, Prebish 1977, Lancaster 1981, and Lamotte 1981.

29. References Dayal 1932: 248, 373 n. 578; Conze 1967 s.v. *upāyakauśalya*. Cp. *Kp* 6v, 42, 48 (*jñāna-upāyakauśalya*).

30. Hikata (1958) and Conze (1960) independently conclude that *PWA* is earlier than *PWP*. Conze was at one time not certain that *Rg* precedes *PWA*, and described *Rg* 29-31 as "filling the gap" left by the story of Sadāprarudita (1968: 169); later he decided that these chapters are a later stratum (1968a:130 *PWA*, p. x). Skill in means is not elaborated at length in *PWA*, as we have observed in Section 2 above; Hikata observes, "it seems that detailed demonstration... was still beyond the scope of the Smaller Sūtra" (1958:xxxi). On *Rg* see also Yuyama 1976. For a table of correspondences between *Rg* and *PWA*, see Conze 1968: 179-82.

31. The Lokakṣema version is more elaborate than later versions; see the study of this story at Lancaster 1974.

32. The relationship of mendicants with female householders—their principal alms-givers—has generally been a topic of absorbing interest to the mendicants; see Frauwallner 1956:124-25, *Lotus* ch. 14, Paul 1979:8.

33. A suggestion for further research: the *Pañcapāramitā-nirdeśa*, T 220:11-15, K 1:11-15=O 848, Toh 181.

34. The treatment of the Buddha by *Up*, Sections Two and Three, appears as Chapter 16 of the *Lotus*, and in *Vk* as the conclusion of chapter 2. See also the *Detachment from the World* section of the Avataṁsaka collection, translated Cleary 1986.

35. See *Mv* 3 (the *Nalinī* and other *jātakas*), O'Flaherty 1973:8-11.

36. See Tatz 1986:211-18. For summaries of *śāstra* discussion of skill in means, see Lamotte 1976:19n.

37. *Up* sections 20, 22, 30, 33, 35, 45 and 57 (two passages). Divisions and subtitles are mine. Reference is made to *Up* also by Prajñākaramati (*Pañjikā* 70), Ratnākaraśānti (O 5331, P 283a1), and Abhayākaragupta (O 5299, P 88a3-4). Pāsādika 1982:103 notes a citation in the *Sūtrasamuccaya.*

38. Done at Tun-huang; completed month 6, day 17 of 285 A.D. See Tsukamoto 1985:208, 215.

39. On Fa-ch'eng see Tatz 1978:20-22 and references. On his translation of the *Laṅkāvatāra* see Takasaki 1978: 459-67. On his rendering of technical terms see Inaba 1977. Among Tibetan indexes, only that of the Sde-dge edition names the translator of the *Up.* The Ratnakūṭa collection contains other translations by Chos-grub; see Lalou 1927:239-40.

On the date of catalogue of Ldan-dkar see Tatz 1978:32, n. 171 and references.

40. The Narthang edition (Lalou 1927:256) gives Jinamitra and Surendrabodhi as Indian informants, but that colophon belongs to the following item, Ratnakūṭa 39.

41. Prior to *Mhv*, because Tibetan no. 2 does not follow *Mhv* exactly; see e.g. the translation at n. 81 below. Completion of the *Mhv* may be ca 824; see references Lamotte 1976:xxxvii note.

42. Thanks to the British Library, and in particular to Chime Tulku, Tibetan Section, Oriental Collections, for providing a print of this.

43. See for example the two Tibetan versions of the *Rāṣṭrapāla-paripṛcchā*, ed. and tr. Ensink 1952; Lalou 1927:242-43; the *Vk* as tr. Lamotte 1976. On the Ratnakūṭa collection see also Pederson 1980, 1979 in *BTI.* Pederson's suggestion that the Ratnakūṭa was collected in China is contradicted by the presence in Tibetan of portions, including title and colophons, translated from Sanskrit. Central Asia must be admitted to be a remote possibility, inasmuch as some translators came to Tibet from Nepal and Central India.

44. The Tibetan translation of *Up* found in *SS* differs from that of the sūtra, but does not indicate any difference from the original of Fa. A older translation of the *SS* done from a different original is attested by Tibetan scholars of the fifteenth century, but has since been lost; see Tatz 1986:170, 177-78, 213, 245.

THE SKILL IN MEANS SŪTRA[1]

Salutations to Buddhas and Bodhisattvas!

PART ONE

THE SKILL IN MEANS OF BODHISATTVAS

The Setting

1. Thus have I heard at one time. The Lord dwelt at Śrāvastī in the Jeta Grove, Anāthapiṇḍada's park, together with the great community of monks consisting of eight thousand monks—those who were yet in training and those who were adepts. There were also sixteen thousand Bodhisattvas, great heroes who were each and all well known for supernatural knowledge, who had mastered the incantations, and whose eloquence had no hindrance, who were skilled in calling forth supernatural knowledge, who had obtained conviction that phenomena are unarising—Bodhisattvas with many hundreds of thousands of good qualities.[2]

2. As the Lord emerged from seclusion, he was encircled by many hundreds of thousands in attendance. He prepared to teach the doctrine. He prepared to reveal the clean; the wholesome at the beginning, the wholesome in the middle, the wholesome at the end; the good content, the good expression; the unadulterated, the complete, the pure, the refined.

The Question

3. At that time the Bodhisattva great hero Jñānottara joined the circle and sat down. Then the Bodhisattva great hero Jñānottara rose from his seat, threw his robe over one shoulder, and placed his right knee to the ground. Bowing, palms joined, towards the Lord, he made this request:

"If the Lord (*bhagavān*) should grant me the opportunity to ask a question to be answered, I would question the Lord the Thus-Come-One, the Worthy, the fully perfected Buddha (*tathāgata-arhat-samyaksambuddha*) upon a certain matter."

The Lord responded to the Bodhisattva great hero Jñānottara: "Son of the family (*kulaputra*), ask the Thus-Come-One whatever question you desire, and I will gratify you with an answer to it."

4. The Bodhisattva, the great hero Jñānottara asked this of the Lord: "Venerable Lord, the Bodhisattva great heroes have something known as skill in means. What is that 'skill in means'? Venerable Lord, how are Bodhisattva great heroes 'skilled in means'?"

5. And the Lord spoke thus to the Bodhisattva, the great hero Jñānottara:

"Son of the family, well and good! Carry on, son of the family, and you will promote good for many people, well-being for many people, sympathy for the world, and welfare, benefit, well-being, and the knowledge of present and future Bodhisattva great heroes for masses of divine and human beings.[3] You will fulfill all the qualities of Buddhahood. You will promote the holy doctrine of Lord Buddhas of the past, the future and the present. Son of the family, for you to think of questioning the Thus-Come-One on the skill in means of Bodhisattvas—that, O son of the family, is well and good of you.

"Let you therefore listen well, son of the family, and be attentive, and I will explain to you the skill in means of Boddhisattva great heroes."

The Answer

6. The Bodhisattva, the great hero Jñānottara said: "Yes, Lord"; he heeded the Lord and the Lord spoke thus to him:

"Son of the family: the Bodhisattva great hero who is skilled in means can fill sentient beings with a single morsel of food.[4] How can this be so? Son of the family, the Bodhisattva great hero who is skilled in means, when he performs the mere act of giving a single morsel of food to an animal, performs that act of giving with an aspiration for omniscience, and he dedicates the store of merit to the fulfillment of the qualities of Buddhahood by all sentient beings.[5]

"There are two reasons that [6]it fills[6] all sentient beings: the aspiration for omniscience and the skilfulness in dedication.

"Son of the family, this is the skill in means of a Bodhisattva great hero.

7. "Son of the family, the Bodhisattva great hero who is skilled in means appreciates others' creation of stores of merit, and he dedicates the merit from that appreciation as well to all sentient beings,

transferring it to them—he performs a further act of dedication. With the merit of having dedicated it to omniscience,

He performs an act of giving with the thought of omniscience, and he outshines those who give without the thought of awakening; he outshines any great patrons; he outshines even any of the recipients.[7] Son of the family, that also is the skill in means of Bodhisattva great heroes.

8. "Son of the family: the Bodhisattva great hero who is skilled in means will mentally find, gather, and present to all the Buddhas any

flowering trees and incense trees, flower garlands, incense, aromatic powders, and unguents to be found in all directions

tree-grown flowers to be found in all directions that are unowned, and incense trees in all directions lightly borne by a breeze

that do not belong to anyone, that are unowned. And the merit stored by this he transfers to all sentient beings, and having renounced it, he dedicates it to omniscience.

"The Bodhisattva who is skilled in means will also present to all the Buddhas the fragrance, borne by a breeze, of any flowering trees, incense trees, flowers, flower garlands, incense, aromatic powders, and unguents to be found in all directions that belong to someone, that are owned. And the merit stored by this he dedicates to the fulfillment of omniscience by himself and all sentient beings.

"By dedicating the store of merit to omniscience, he will obtain measureless aggregates of morality, concentration, wisdom, liberation, and liberated intuitive-vision.[8] Son of the family, that also is the skill in means of a Bodhisattva great hero.

9. "Son of the family: the Bodhisattva great hero who is skilled in means [9]appreciates the collective[9] well-being experienced by sentient beings in the realm of the universe of all directions. He dedicates the appreciation to omniscience.

"He exposes[10] the collective feelings of suffering experienced by sentient beings in the realms of the universe of all directions. He fortifies himself thus: 'May all the feelings of suffering of those sentient beings fall upon myself! May they be well!'

"Because he now generates a thought that has omniscience as its object, he will in future alleviate all the suffering of all sentient beings. He dedicates the appreciation to omniscience, and the merit stored by that will result in the obtainment of everything that makes for well-being on the level of a Buddha. Son of the family, that also is the skill in means of a Bodhisattva great hero.

And he dedicates the merit stored by that as well to awakening.

10. "Son of the family: the Bodhisattva great hero who is skilled in means, when he makes salutation, pays respect, displays reverence, does honor, worships, and serves a single Thus-Come-One, considers himself to be making salutation, paying respect, displaying reverence, doing honor, worshiping, and serving all Thus-Come-Ones. He trains himself to think thus:

" 'The Lord Buddhas evolve from the same element of dharma;

" 'All Buddhas have one element of dharma;

they have the same morality, the same concentration, and the same wisdom, the same liberation and the same liberated intuitive-vision;[11] the same knowledge and the same understanding.'

"The Bodhisattva who is skilled in means

"Skilled in means, he pays respect to all Buddhas in paying respect to one Buddha; he

mentally procures anything that would serve as an offering to the Lord Buddhas of infinity, and then he makes a dedication to omniscience. Son of the family, that also is the skill in means of the Bodhisattva great hero.

11. "Son of the family: the Budhisattva great hero who is skilled in means does not discount himself when he is dull-witted,

nor is he discouraged (*na samilīyate*).

but extols himself[12] (*ātmānam praśaṁsate*).

Reciting but a single four-line stanza, he considers that the meaning of the stanza comprises the sense of all the Word of the Buddha. He practices recitation of the stanza and, without being discoursed, generating great compassion and having no desire for gain, respect, or fame, he makes the following resolve:

" 'I will expound this stanza in detail to masses of people in village, town, and market, in the countryside and in the capital.' And he resolves:

" 'May all sentient beings who hear this four-line stanza of mine

be assured of supreme, right and full awakening (*anuttarasamyaksambodhi-niyata*).'

" 'The store of merit thus acquired by skill in means will result in his becoming as erudite as any sentient being—including Ānanda—and obtaining the very eloquence of a Buddha. That also is the skill in means of a Bodhisattva great hero."

obtain the eloquence of a Buddha (*buddhapratibhānalabdha*).'

"That store of merit outshines the boundless, incomparable erudition of any sentient being, and obtains the very eloquence of a Buddha.

12. "Son of the family: the Bodhisattva great hero who is skilled in means, in the rare instance when he is impoverished, performs the deeds of others at least to some extent.[13] Without being discouraged, he takes something as slight as a spoonful of food and presents it to a monastic or an ordinary person.

"In giving it, he considers: 'The Lord has said that gifts become great when given with great thoughts. I may have only a little something to give, but given with the thought of omniscience, it is measureless.'

13. "He gives something as slight as a spoonful of food with that measureless thought of omniscience[14] and dedicates it, thinking,

" 'By this store of merit of mine, may I and all sentient beings come to have the most excellent taste (a mark of the superman) and come to have a jewel in hand— like the Lord, the Thus-Come-One, the Worthy, the full and perfect Buddha Śākyamuni.'[15]

"'May all sentient beings become like the present Thus-Come-One 'Jewel in Hand'.

"The dedication of that store of merit to omniscience outshines the meritorious work of giving on the part of sentient beings who lack the thought of awakening.[16] Son of the family, that also is the skill in means of a Bodhisattva great hero.

"That little spoonful of food accomplishes meritorious work that is essentially identical to giving, morality, and meditational development.

14. "Son of the family: the Bodhisattva great hero who is skilled in means may live together with auditors and Independent Buddhas,[17] but he is not pleased with them. If he the Bodhisattva who is skilled in means should see that they are excessively esteemed in relation to himself, he draws two contrasts with himself. What are the two contrasts? He thinks:

"'First, the lord Buddhas evolve from Bodhisattvas, and the auditors and Independent Buddhas evolve from Buddhas. When they are excessively esteemed, I myself am being esteemed foremost: I am chief, and not they. Secondly, they are using my father's accumulated wealth: Let me be neither pleased with, nor envious of them.'[18]

15. "No one who resolutely generates the thought will be puffed-up even if he be esteemed by someone as a Thus-Come-One, nor will he be discouraged at not being esteemed. He will succeed in eliminating both affection and resentment—in effect, adopting even mindedness toward all sentient beings. Son of the family, that also is the skill in means of the Bodhisattva great hero.

16. "Son of the family: the Bodhisattva great hero who is skilled in means fulfills all six perfections in giving a gift. How does he fulfill them? The Bodhisattva great hero who is skilled in means, when a beggar comes before him, suppresses stinginess—making omniscience his mental object—and develops a strong sense of renunciation, engendering the intention to give: this is his perfection of giving.

"He gives to those who have undertaken and keeps a vow of ethics; he impels the immoral to be moral and gives them a gift, thus projecting them to supreme, right and full awakening: this is his perfection of morality.[19]

17. "Giving a gift with thoughts that are loving, benevolent, unfeigned, unagitated, not apathetic, upolluted, and absorbed: this is his perfection of patience.

"He performs a welcoming salutation to those who are to eat and drink, whether they are persons who drink, lick, or otherwise consume;[20] he makes effort; he serves with body and he serves with mind; he rises, he comes, and he goes: this is his perfection of vigor.

"He raises body, speech, and mind for those who are to eat, drink, or otherwise consume; he comes and he goes: this is his perfection of vigor.

"In any act of giving his thinking is one-pointed; his attitude is elated, happy, and jubilant; he is free from mental wandering: this is his perfection of meditation.

"Giving a gift he does not grasp at anything, but is one-pointed and refreshed:[21] this is his perfection of meditation.

18. "Giving a gift, he focuses his attention (*samanvāharati*) upon the nature of things (*dharmatā*). He thinks: 'Who performs the giving? To whom does he give? What is given? Who will enjoy the karmic reward for it?' He searches in this way, but cannot envisage any phenomenon (*dharma*) that performs the act of giving, to whom something is given, that is given, or who will enjoy a karmic reward. This is his perfection of wisdom.

"Giving a gift, his point of reference (*pratisaraṇa*) is the nature of things. He thinks: 'Who gives this? Who eats it? Who will enjoy the karmic reward?' He searches in that way, but cannot envisage any phenomenon that performs the act of giving, to who something is given, or who will enjoy a karmic reward. This is his perfection of wisdom.

"Son of the family, this is how the Bodhisattva great hero who is skilled in means fulfills all six perfections in giving a gift."

19. Then the Bodhisattva great hero Jñānottara said this to the Lord: "Venerable Lord, such skill in means of Bodhisattva great heroes is amazing. The very giving by which other sentient beings are kept in saṁsāra enables the Bodhisattva great hero who is skilled in means to acquire the qualities of Buddhahood."[22]

The Lord replied: "That is how it is. Son of the family, what you have said is so. The Bodhisattva great hero who is skilled in means with skill in means and the perfection of skill in means accomplishes a great deal with just a little giving. With much giving, his accomplishment is measureless and incalculable."

What is Moral Transgression for a Bodhisattva?

20. Then the Lord said to the Bodhisattva great hero Jñānottara:

"Son of the family:[23] the Bodhisattva who is skilled in means attenuates even a grave transgression with skill in means. How does he do so?

"Son of the family: the Bodhisattva great hero who is skilled in means, on the rare occasion upon which a transgression befalls him because he is under the influence of an unwholesome adviser or because he is confused, will consider the matter thus:

"'Let me not enter nirvāṇa with these aggregates, elements, and sense-fields in any case, lest I burn with anxiety.[24] Instead, let me prepare myself to remain in saṁsāra until its future end, in order to bring sentient beings to maturity. Let me not be discouraged, fearful or anxious: As long as I continue to samsarize as recompense for that transgression, I will bring sentient beings to maturity. Besides, I will be bound that it not recur. Moreover, I will teach doctrine to all sentient beings in order that they be extricated from transgression.'

"Suppose, son of the family, that a Bodhisattva who is a monastic should fall into all four seminal transgressions.[25] If he removed them with this skill in means, I would call it no transgression on the part of the Bodhisattva."

[*SS* 93:23-29: *iha kulaputra upāyakuśalo bodhisattvo yadā kadācit kasmiṁścit pāpamitra vaśenāpattim āpadyet, sa itaḥ pratisaṁśikṣate—na mayaibhiḥ skandhaiḥ parinirvāpayitavyam/ mayā punar evaṁ samnāhaḥ saṁnaddhavyaḥ—aparāntakotiḥ saṁsaritavyā sattvānaṁ paripācanahetor iti/ na mayā cittadāhaḥ karaṇīyaḥ/ yathā yathā saṁsariṣyāmi tathā tathā sattvān paripācayiṣyāmi/ api tvetāṁ cāpattiṁ yathā dharmaṁ parikariṣyāmi/ ātyatyāṁ saṁvaram āpatsye/ sacet kulaputra pravrajito bodhisattvaḥ parikalpamādāya sarvāś catasro mūlāpattir atikramet, anena copāyakauśalyena vinodayet, anāpattim bodhiṣattvasya vadāmi//*]

21. Then the Bodhisattva, the great hero Jñānottara asked this of the Lord: "Venerable Lord, when is a Bodhisattva possessed of transgression?"

22. The Lord replied [26]to the Bodhisattva the great hero Jñānottara:[26]

"Suppose, son of the family, that a Bodhisattva were to train himself in the prātimokṣa training, subsisting on roots and fruit for a hundred thousand eons, patiently enduring the approbation as well as the scorn of all sentient beings.[27] Yet, if he were to adjust himself to concerns associated with the stage of [Skt] auditors and Independent Buddhas—that,

O son of the family, would be what is known as a seminal transgression of the utmost gravity for a Bodhisattva.

"By analogy, son of the family, if someone of the vehicle of the auditors incurs a seminal transgression, he loses the opportunity to enter nirvāṇa with those aggregates, elements, and sense-fields. In the same way, [28]son of the family,[28] so long as the Bodhisattva fails to confess his fault and to eliminate auditor and Independent Buddha-like concerns, he loses the opportunity to enter nirvāṇa

understood as supreme, right and full awakening; he loses the opportunity to attain the stage of a Buddha. It becomes impossible."

at the stage of a Buddha."[29]

[*SS* 40:25-30: *kim cāpi kulaputra bodhisattvaḥ prātimokṣa-śikṣāyām śikṣamāṇaḥ kalpasataśahasram api mūlaphalabhakṣaḥ syāt/ sarvasattvānāṁ ca sūktaduruktāni kṣamet/ śrāvakapratyekabuddha-bhūmipratisaṁyuktaiśca manasikārair viharet/ iyaṁ bodhisattvasya gurukā mūlāpattiḥ/ tadyathā kulaputra śrāvakayānīyo mūlāpattim āpannaḥ, so 'bhavyas tair eva skandhaiḥ parinirvātum, evam eva kulaputro 'pratideśyaitām āpattim aniḥsṛjya tān śrāvakapratyekabuddha-manasikārān, abhavyo buddhabhūmau parinirvātum//*]

The Bodhisattva and Sexuality: The Bodhisattva "King at the Head of the Masses"

23. Then the master Ānanda said to the Lord:[30]

"Venerable Lord, the Thus-Come-One may be the teacher of all sentient beings; and it may be that there is nothing not known to, not seen and realized by, not directly evident to him. Nevertheless, the Thus-Come-One has said, 'When you see a monk incur a transgression, do not dissemble, but tell your fellow celibates or the Thus-Come-One.[31] Therefore I relate this to the Lord, with friendliness and the intention of avoiding an act of transgression.

"Venerable Lord, as I was making my round for alms in this great city of Śrāvastī,

"Lord, as I was making my round for alms, I saw the Bodhisattva King at the Head of the Masses in a certain house, together with a woman on the same couch. The Lord has said, 'When you see a transgression occur do not dissemble, but tell your fellow celibates or the Thus-Come-One.' The Thus-Come-One is the teacher of all sentient beings; there is nothing not known to, not seen and realized by the Thus-Come-One—that is why I relate this to the Lord."

I saw the Bodhisattva King at the Head of the
Masses inside a certain house, together with
a woman on a couch."

When master Ānanda had finished speaking, the great earth suddenly shook in six ways.[32]

24. Then the Bodhisattva King at the Head of Masses levitated and sat in the atmosphere before the Lord at seven times the height of a palm tree. Addressing master Ānanda, he said: "Master Ānanda, what do you think of this? Can someone sit in the atmosphere while possessed of a subject of transgression?"

Ānanda answered, "No, son of the family, he cannot."[33]

The Bodhisattva King at the Head of the Masses asked again: "Then let master Ānanda ask the Thus-Come-One who is present before us now how one comes to be possessed of a subject of Bodhisattva transgression."[34]

Master Ānanda was disconcerted. Bowing his head to the feet of the Lord, he said to the Lord:

"Venerable Lord, I disclose as an offense the offense I have committed in accusing such a standard-bearer of a fault. May it please the Lord to accept as an offense the offense I have confessed as an offense."[35]

25. The Lord replied to master Ānanda: "Ānanda, do not conceive of a holy person, someone practicing the Greater Vehicle correctly, as being faulty. Ānanda, this is how you should understand it: A person of the vehicle of the auditors, in order to be absolutely peerless in maintaining meditative calm, will seek uninterruptedly to exhaust the outflows. In the same way, Ānanda, the Bodhisattva great hero who is skilled in means, who is endowed with the thought of omniscience, will seek uninterruptedly for omniscience, even to the point of abiding among a holy retinue of women and enjoying, playing with, and taking pleasure in it.[36]

"Why so? Ānanda, the Bodhisattva great hero who is skilled in means takes a retinue only to introduce it to the three jewels—the jewel of the Buddha, the jewel of the doctrine and the jewel of the community—and to supreme, right and full awakening.

"Ānanda, if you should see a son of the family or a daughter of the family (someone of the Bodhisattva vehicle) who, while not parted from the thought of omniscience, is enjoying, playing with and taking pleasure in the five sensuous qualities—then, Ānanda, you should understand that the holy person in question is endowed with five faculties like those of the Thus-Come-One.[37]

26. "Now listen, Ānanda, to why the Bodhisattva King at the Head of the Masses was sitting together with a woman on a couch. That woman,

Ānanda, had been the wife of Bodhisattva King at the Head of the Masses for the past

five hundred lives. Because of that clumsiness (*ayoniśa*)[38] in the past, her thoughts clung to that son of the family. On the other hand, she perceived the splendor and majesty (generated by the power of his past morality) of the Bodhisattva King at the Head of the Masses. She found herself incapable of uttering the lewd words that would take her to (*sic*) a lower rebirth.

two hundred lives. Because of that tendency latent (*anuśaya*) from the past, she perceived the splendor and majesty (generated by the power of his past morality) of the son of the family, the Bodhisattva King at the Head of the Masses. Defilement arose, and she uttered lewd words that would take her to a lower rebirth.

"Off in private, the thought arose in her mind, 'If the Bodhisattva King at the Head of the Masses were to sit with me on a couch, I also would generate the thought of supreme, right and full awakening.'

27. "Ānanda,[39] the Bodhisattva King at the Head of the Masses cognized that sister's supposition with his mind.

He let the night pass and in the morning put on his under and outer robes, took his bowl and went for alms to the great city of Śrāvastī. Wandering through the great city of Śrāvastī for alms, he came to the house of that sister.

He let the night pass and then came to her house.

"He thought about the earth-equivalency—the spiritual exercise of equating the internal and external elements of earth.[40] He took that sister by the right hand, and they sat down on a couch. As soon as they had been seated, he spoke this stanza:

The Buddha does not praise desire;
That is the range of the foolish.
Eliminate craving for sense-objects,
And become the best of humanity—a Buddha.

28. "Ānanda, then that sister, hearing the stanza, was elated and jubilant. She rose from the couch and fell at the feet of the Bodhisattva King at the Head of the Masses. Then she uttered these stanzas:

Desires censured by the Buddha,
I will not seek hereafter;
Abandoning thirst for sense-objects,
I'll become the best humanity—a Buddha.

The offensive thought I was thinking,

I hereby confess to you;
For the welfare of [41]all living creatures,
I generate the wish for awakening.

29. "Ānanda, the Bodhisattva King at the Head of the Masses instructed that sister in supreme, right and full awakening, built her up to it, introduced her to it, and established her in it with that skill in means. Then he rose from the couch and departed.

"Ānanda, regard the distinction of his beneficent intentions! Ānanda, I make this prediction in regard to that sister: Upon transmigrating from here, she will exchange her woman's body. After 9.9 million 'incalculable' eons, she will become and appear in the world as a Thus-Come-One, a Worthy, a fully perfected Buddha named Free From Obsession. In the Buddha-field in which he obtains awakening, sentient beings will have no unwholesome obsession at all in their minds.[42]

"Ānanda, you may understand by this account how a Bodhisattva takes a retinue without its becoming a subject of transgression."

30. Then the Bodhisattva King at the Head of the Masses descended from the atmosphere. He made a prostration to the Lord, and said:

"Venerable Lord, a Bodhisattva maintains skill in means and great compassion. Venerable Lord, this is how I think of it:

"Suppose that a transgression would befall a Bodhisattva in the course of creating a store of merit for a particular sentient being, and the offense would cause him to burn in hell for a hundred thousand eons. The Bodhisattva will incur the transgression—and the suffering of hell—enthusiastically, O Venerable Lord, rather than relinquish the store of merit of a single sentient being."[43]

[*SS* 93:20-23: *yadi bodhisattva ekasya sattvasya kuśalamūlaṁ saṁjanayet tathārūpāṁ cāpattim āpadyeta yathārūpayā āpattyā āpannayā kalpaśatasahasraṁ niraye pacyeta, utsoḍhavyam eva bhagavan bodhisattavenāpattim āpattuṁ tacca nairayikaṁ duḥkham/ na tveva tasyaikasya sattvasya kuśalaṁ paritayaktum//*]

31. The Lord gave a "Well done!" to the Bodhisattva King at the Head of the Masses. "Well done, well done, holy personage. With such great compassion, a Bodhisattva avoids any transgression; he possesses no subject of transgression. How is this the case?

The Bodhisattva and Sexuality: The Story of Jyotis

32. "Son of the family, this I know for myself. Once upon a time, incalculably more long ago than an 'incalculable' eon, vastly, immeasurably, inconceivably long ago, there was a brahman youth named Jyotis. He practiced celibacy in the woods for forty-two thousand years. When those forty-two thousand years had passed, he came to a capital named Surāṣṭra. As he entered the great city, the brahman youth's fine figure, beauty, and attractiveness was noticed by a female water-carrier. She ran up to the youth and threw herself before him with her mind obsessed by lust.[44]

33. "Son of the family, Jyotis the brahman youth then said to the woman,[45] 'Sister, what do you want?'

"She answered him, 'Brahman youth, I seek you.'

"He said to her, 'Sister, I am not eager for sense-pleasures. I am celibate.'

"She said to him, 'Brahman youth, if I cannot be with you, I will die.'

"Jyotis the brahman youth thought to himself, 'It is not right for me to break my vow of austerity (*vrata*) today, after having kept celibacy for forty-two thousand years.' He pulled himself forcibly away, rejecting the woman, and fled. He was seven steps away when compassion was born in him. He thought:

" 'I may go to hell for breaking my vow of austerity. But I can bear to experience the pain of hell. Let this woman not die, but be happy.'[46]

"Son of the family, Jyotis the brahman youth returned. Taking the woman by the right hand, he said, 'Sister, arise. I will do whatever you desire.'

[*SS* 93:14-17: *saptame pade sthitasya kāruṇyam utpadyeta/ kiṃ cāpy aham idaṁ vrataṁ khaṇḍayitvā nirayaparāyanaḥ syām, tathāpy utsahe 'ham nairayikaṁ duḥkhaṁ prativedyayitum/ atha ceyaṁ strī sukhitā bhavatu/ mā kālaṁ karotu/ 'iti hi kulaputra jyotir māṇavakaḥ paścānmukho nivartya tāṁ striyaṁ dakṣiṇena pāṇinā gṛhītvaivam āha—uttiṣṭha bhagini yathākāma karaṇīyas te bhavāmitti//*]

34. "Jyotis the brahman youth lived the home life for twelve years before leaving it again to generate the four stations of brahma. When he died, he was immediately reborn in the world of Brahmā."[47]

35. "Son of the family: At that time, in that life, I was none other than Jyotis the brahman youth. Do not view it otherwise. Have no second thoughts or doubt on this point. Yaśodharā was the female water-carrier.

"Son of the family: Because I generated a thought that was endowed with great compassion but conjoined with transitory passion, birth-and-death was curtailed for ten thousand eons.[48]

"Son of the family, take note: Something that sends other sentient beings to hell, sends the Bodhisattva who is skilled in means to rebirth in the world of Brahmā."

[*SS* 93:17-19: *so 'ham kulaputra mahākāruṇyacittotpādenetvareṇa kāmopasaṁhitena daśakalpasahasrāṇi* [49]*saṁsāraṁ*[49] *akārṣaṃ/ paśya kulaputra yad anyeṣāṁ nirayasaṁvartanīyaṁ karma, tad upāyakauśalyasya bodhisattvasya brahmalokopapattisaṁvartanīyam//*]

The Bodhisattva and Sexuality: The Story of Vimala

36. Then the Lord again addressed the Bodhisattva great hero Jñānottara:

"Son of the family: If the monks Śāriputra and Maudgalyāyana had been skilled in means, the monk Kokālika would not have gone to hell. Why so?[50]

37. "Son of the family, this I know for myself. Once upon a time, during the promulgation of the Thus-Come-One, the Worthy, the fully perfected Buddha Kakutsunda,[51] there was a monk a preacher of doctrine named Vimala ('Immaculate') who dwelt in a remote cave. Not far from him lived five hundred ṛṣis. During that period a mass of clouds arose unseasonably, and a great rain came to fall. A pair of women who were *en route* between villages entered Vimala's cave seeking refuge from the rain. When they re-emerged from the cave, they were spied by the five hundred ṛṣis. Seeing them, the five hundred ṛṣis thought
harsh and hateful thoughts: in alarm:

"'Aha! This monk Vimala is lusting for wickedness. He is uncelibate.'

38. "Then the monk Vimala, knowing in his mind the thinking of those five hundred ṛṣis, levitated into the atmosphere to seven times the height of a palm tree. Seeing him sitting there, the ṛṣis thought to themselves:

"'According to our theories, someone who is uncelibate cannot levitate and sit in the atmosphere.'

"Without further ado they made prostration with five limbs to the feet of the monk Vimala and confessed their fault to be a fault.

"Son of the family: If the monk Vimala had not levitated and sat in the atmosphere at that time, those five hundred ṛṣis would have fallen physically into hell.[52]

39. "Son of the family, what do you think of this? At that time, in that life the present Bodhisatta Maitreya was none other than the monk Vimala.[53] Do not view it otherwise. Have no second thoughts or doubt on this point.

"Son of the family: You should understand by this account that if the monks Śāriputra and Maudgalyāyana had levitated and sat in the atmosphere, the monk Kokālika would not have gone to hell.

Illustrations of Bodhisattva Gnosis

40. "Son of the family: You should also understand, by the above account, that the gnosis of the Bodhisattva who is skilled in means, whatever it turns towards,

is beyond the stage (*bhūmi*)

is beyond the range (*viṣaya*)

of auditors and independent Buddhas.[54]

41. "Son of the family, he is like a courtesan who is learned and proficient in the sixty-four arts. Desiring money,

she will yield herself and give pleasure to a man and not withhold anything necessary until she has obtained everything that she wants from him.

she will yield and display her body to a man and not withhold anything necessary until she has obtained money from him.

And after she has obtained what she wants she will ignore him and reject him, not giving him another thought, and she will have no regard for him at all.[55]

"In the same way, son of the family, the Bodhisattva who is skilled in means knows how to bring sentient beings to maturity with that skill in means.

As in the above example, he adapts himself to the dispositions of sentient beings, nor does he withhold anything that is necessary for them. He takes pleasure in the virtue of sentient beings, and in doing so he surrenders himself; but it is not the case that he enjoys what happens to be necessary. When the time comes that he knows, 'At last, these sentient beings have developed stores of merit, and cannot lose them in future,' he proceeds to ignore and reject all sense-pleasure and games, leaving them without another thought.

He takes pleasure in the stores of merit of sentient beings, and in doing so he withholds nothing, and he adapts himself to sentient beings until he has displayed the yielding of his own body. When the time comes that he knows, 'At last, these sentient beings have developed stores of merit, and there is nothing more that I can do for them,' he proceeds to ignore them, leaving them without another thought.

42. "Son of the family: He is like a bee (the creature of the animal class of rebirth). Although he smells and tastes all the flowers, the bee

never develops a notion of their permanence, nor does he allow himself to develop a craving for them to remain.

does not develop a craving for permanence in them.

He does not try to steal the scent from them, or the leaves, the stalk, or the flowers.

"In the same way, son of the family, the Bodhisattva who is skilled in means indulges himself in all manner of sensual pleasure and games in order to bring sentient beings to maturity, without

developing any notion of permanence in them, nor allowing himself to generate a craving for them to remain.	generating any craving for permanence in them.

Nor does he wound himself or anyone else.

43. "Son of the family, he is like a seed burned by fire: it does not lose its character (*varṇa*), even if it lacks the opportunity to sprout. In the same way, son of the family,

when a Bodhisattva's defilements have been burned by the perfection of the wisdom of emptiness, signlessness, wishlessness, and self-lessness, he does not possess himself of defilement that leads to great distress, even if he should indulge himself in all manner of sensual pleasure; nor does he lose the character of Buddhahood.[56]	because he has cultivated the wisdom of emptiness, signlessness, and wishlessness, he indulges himself in all manner of pleasure and games but does not possess himself of defilement that leads to great distress; nor does he lose the qualities of Buddhahood.

44. "Son of the family, he is like an expert fisherman. The fisherman puts an unbaited hook on a line and casts it into a great lake. He draws whatever he desires from the great lake, whenever he so desires with that single well-guarded line.

"In the same way, son of the family, the Boddhisattva who is skilled in means will focus his thought firmly on omniscience, cultivating the perfection of the wisdom of emptiness, signlessness, and wishlessness and self-lessness. He enters the great swamp of sense-desire but he will be reborn in the world of Brahmā, rejecting the realm of sense-desire, whenever he so desires, but guarding well that thought of omniscience.

45. "Son of the family, he is like

a man bearing spells and mantras. The king's men (*vidyāmantradharaḥ puruṣaiḥ*)	a man bearing mantric spells. The king (*mantravidyādharaḥ puruṣo rājñā*)

may seize and bind him with a bond of five ropes, but he will go wherever he desires, whenever he so desires, cutting the bonds by once generating the force of the

spells and mantras.	mantric spells.

"In the same way, son of the family, the Bodhisattva who is skilled in means will take pleasure in the five kinds of sense-qualities in order to bring sentient beings to maturity; he will allow himself to be permeated by them. Yet, he will cut through all the bonds of sense-qualities whenever he so desires and transmigrate from there to be reborn in the world of Brahmā

by generating the force of the spell and mantra of wisdom and by once guarding well the thought of omniscience.

by a single thought of omniscience generated by the force of the spell of wisdom.[57]

[*SS* 92:15-19: *tadyathā kulaputra mantravidyādharaḥ puruṣo rājñā pañcapāśakena bandhanena baddhaḥ syāt/ sa yadā kāṅkṣeta prakramanāya, tadaikamantravidyābalena sarvabandhanāni chitvā prakramet/ evam eva kulaputra upāyakuśalo bodhisattvaḥ pañcabhiḥ kāmaguṇaiḥ ratiṁ vindati, taiścākīrno viharati/ yadā ca punar ākāṅksate, tadā prajñābalādhinena ekena ca sarvajñatācittena sarvakāmaguṇān prabhujya cyuto brahmaloka upapadyate//*]

46. "Son of the family, he is like a seasoned warrior.[58] Armed with sharp weapons concealed in cloth, he sets out to escort a company of travellers. Some sentient beings among them, being ignorant that he knows weaponry, pity the warrior; they think contemptuous thoughts of him, and they say:

"'He has no bow

nor sword, nor arrow.

nor any other weapon.

He has no companions. He cannot defend this company of travellers. He cannot defend even himself: how can he defend all the travellers and defeat a company of bandits? It is impossible. He will end in disaster (*anaya-vyasanam*).'

"Then the warrior goes into the wilderness. A band of robbers attacks. He ruthlessly arms himself with his weapons. Raising his weapons, he fires them at the bandits and slays them all. Then he puts his weapons away again.

47. "In the same way, son of the family, the Bodhisattva

who is skilled in means

great hero

ruthlessly wields his weapons of the perfection of wisdom in order to bring sentient beings to maturity. With skill in means, he indulges in pleasure and play with the five kinds of sense-desire. Some individuals of the auditors' vehicle

who do not fathom his knowledge of skill in means, see him

see his physical faculties

and lack faith in him. They pity him and say:

"'This person, living in a state of carelessness, cannot even save himself. How can he save all others and defeat the legion of Māra. It is impossible. He will end in disaster.'[59]

"But the Bodhisattva is possessed of skill in means and wisdom and he can, whenever he so desires, slash all the nets of defilement with his sword of wisdom and betake himself to a purified Buddha-field conjoined with wisdom that is free from

women and licentiousness."

licentious women."

The Bodhisattva and Sexuality Concluded: Priyaṁkara and Dakṣiṇottarā

48. At that time—while that account was being given—a Bodhisattva great hero named Priyaṁkara ("Exhilarating") entered the great city of Śrāvastī for alms. While on his round for alms in the great city of Śrāvastī, he came to the house of a certain wealthy merchant (*śreṣṭhī*). He the merchant had a daughter in the flush of youth named Śrī Dakṣiṇottarā ("Superior Donations") who was on the terrace atop the house. Hearing the call of a monk, she took up some food and brought it out to the Bodhisattva Priyaṁkara.

Then the maid Śrī Dakṣiṇottarā saw the Bodhisattva Priyaṁkara. Immediately, she perceived the features of his beauteous proportions, the sound of his voice, and his complexion[60] with her thoughts possessed by a sexual passion. With her thoughts possesed by passion, aroused by passion, obsessed by passion, burning with passion, her whole body burst into a sweat and while standing there, she died.

49. For his part, the Bodhisattva Priyaṁkara also gave rise to clumsy discursiveness—a thought of sexual passion—upon seeing the maid Śrī Dakṣiṇottarā. At the same moment, however, he became mindful of it, thinking:

"What is the phenomenon (*dharma*) of becoming attached, and what phenomenon is its object? Does the eye become attached to an eye?

But an eye does not become attached: The eye itself is inert, inactive, insentient, conditioned, rigid, a lump of flesh; the eye is inherently empty, hence it does not cognize and it does not feel.[61]

The eye has no feeling; it is inactive, conditioned, a lump of flesh; being inherently empty, it is insensate.

"The same holds for the ear, nose, tongue, body, mind organ, skin, complexion, and flesh."

"Do ear, nose, tongue, body, and mind organ become attached?"

Making analysis in that way from

He could find no phenomenon,

the soles of the feet to the top of the head, he could not find any phenomenon, inside or outside, that could become attached, hateful, or confused. Failing to find anything, his thought of desire-attachment was dispelled.

By correct mental analysis, he came to obtain conviction that phenomena are unarising.

inside or outside, that could become attached or hateful. Failing to find anything, his thought of desire-attachment was dispelled, analyzing the body, covered by skin and flesh, from head to foot.

By correct mental analysis, he comprehended the non-arising of all phenomena and obtained conviction that phenomena are unarising.

With elation and jubilance at that, he was elevated into the atmosphere to seven times the height of a palm tree. Seven times he circled the great city of Śrāvastī. Then he came from the sky to the Jeta Grove and came before the Lord.

50. The Lord saw the Bodhisattva great hero Priyaṁkara coming from the atmosphere, unobstructed like a swan. And having seen him, he said to master Ānanda:

"Ānanda, do you see the Bodhisattva great hero Priyaṁkara coming from the atmosphere, unobstructed like a swan?"

And the answer of Ānanda was, "I do see him, Lord."

The Lord said, "Ānanda: the Bodhisattva great hero Priyaṁkara has analyzed all phenomena in terms of desire-attachment, and in so doing he has tamed the legion of Māra and turned the wheel of doctrine."

51. When the maid Śrī Dakṣiṇottarā died, she transformed her woman's body to obtain a male body and be reborn in paradise among the gods (*deva*) of the Thirty-three. As soon as she had been reborn, a twelve-leagued palace made of the seven precious substances appeared for him.[62] Fourteen thousand goddesses (*apsaras*)

dwelt (*upasthita*) there

were born (*upapatti*) there

to serve him.

52. The thought occurred to him, "What have I done to be reborn here?" Knowledge that is a recollection of past deeds arose in him, and he thought:

"I was the daughter of a merchant in the great city of Śrāvastī, and while there I gazed amorously upon the Bodhisattva great hero Priyaṁkara. After dying with my mind possessed by lust, I transformed my woman's body to obtain a male body here. I have become opulent beyond measure."[63]

Then the male divinity (*devaputra*) thought: "If this be the reward for thoughts of lust, what would be my reward for doing prostrations and service with thoughts of faith to the Bodhisattva great hero Priyaṁkara?[64] It is inappropriate and wrong for me to continue in a state of careless indulgence in sensual exhilaration and play and sexual pleasure. Instead, let me go before the Lord and the Bodhisattva great hero Priyaṁkara."

53. Then that divinity, with his five hundred attendants, went before the Lord and the Bodhisattva great hero Priyaṁkara bearing celestial flowers, incense, garlands, and unguents, with a golden effulgence lighting up the Jeta Grove with a great glow.[65] He made offering to the Lord with the celestial flowers, incense, garlands, and unguents, and he made prostration to the Lord. He made prostration to the Bodhisattva great hero Priyaṁkara, to all the bodhisattva, and to the community of monks. Then he made circumambulation of the Lord three times.[66] Before the Lord, palms joined, he spoke these stanzas:

54.

(1) "The Buddhas, the best of men, are beyond conception,
And seekers of high awakening are beyond conception;
The doctrine of the Thus-Come-One is beyond conception,
And the course of the renowned is beyond conception.

(2) "Once I was a maid in Śrāvastī,
A merchant's daughter, Dakṣiṇā by name,
Beautiful in the initial flush of youth,
Fostered lovingly by my parents.

(3) "An irreproachable son of the Buddha,
Called Priyaṁkara of great might,
While in Śrāvastī seeking alms,
Came to the house of my father.

(4) "When I heard his sweet, pleasing voice,
I willingly took up food,
And came before Priyaṁkara,
Mighty son of the Thus-Come-One.

(5) "My mind was aroused to see him,
With clumsy desire-attachment;
I thought, if I cannot have him as a desire,
I may as well die, indifferent to my life.

(6) "I caught fire with clumsy passion,
And could not speak a single word to him;
Unable even to bestow the alms,
Standing there I sweated right to death.

(7) "At the very instant of my death,
Lord, my woman's body was abandoned;
I was born in paradise by transmigration,
And obtained this luminous body of a male.

(8) "A place of peerless beauty then appeared,
Pleasing to look at, made of precious things,
Filled with fourteen thousand celestial females,
The retinue of servants I obtained.

(9) "Then the wholesome thought occurred to me:[67]
Of what is such maturation the reward?
Remembering, this is what I thought:
Such is the maturation of a thought of lust.

(10) "By looking with a mind possessed of lust
At Priyaṁkara the pleasing, the luminous, the wise,
Such wholesome maturation is reward,
Such majestic power have I.

(11) "If this be the maturation of attachment,
What would come of worshiping him?
This is scarcely the stage of auditors and self-Buddhas,
But leads one toward a *sugata* sort of gnosis.

(12) "Before this victor I hereby resolve
To obtain the highest gnosis of a Buddha;
Coursing for eons as many as sands found in the Ganges,
Let this my obligation never be renounced.

(13) "Priyaṁkara my holy adviser I will worship,
With offerings vast and sublime;[68]
I'll make no offerings to any other guides
Other than those who actively seek awakening.

(14) "May any woman who looks at me,[69]
With thoughts of desire-attachment,
Transform her female body to obtain
The confident form of a man,
And take the highest course of awakening."

55.

(1) The maid's parents, seeing that she had sweat herself to death,
Thought that her life had been expelled
By an ascetic with devil lore;
They wept, and spoke ill of ascetics.[70]

(2) That male divinity, empowered by the Buddha,
Went and spoke with the parents:
"Be not angry with the ascetic,
Lest you incur protracted suffering.

(3) "Your daughter Dakṣiṇottarā who died,
Has been reborn among the Thirty-three;
She has transformed her woman's body,
Into that of a luminous deity, a male.

(4) "Go now before the One Who is Well Gone,
And confess your fault of thinking angry thoughts;
Only in the Buddhas, the best of humanity,
Is there a place for beings to have recourse."

56.

(1) Properly exhorted by this confident one,
Both parents set out to hear the Buddha's word;
With their household and a gathering of kinsmen,
They came into the presence of the Śākya sage.

(2) Prostrating to the feet of the best of men,
They confessed the transgression of having an angry thought;
They taking refuge[71] in the Thus-Come-One,
They asked this of the *Sugata*, the self-existent.

(3) "With how much should we make offering to the Guide,
And with how much to the Doctrine and the Community?
We beg your predication to the question,
And will act according to what it is we hear."

(4) The Victor was aware of their predispositions,
And the World-protector answered in this way:
"Someone who wishes to do worship to all the Buddhas,
Should generate a firm thought for awakening."

(5) The girl's father and her mother and their kinsmen,
All of them no fewer than five hundred,
Heard the promulgation of the man among men,
And generated firm thoughts for awakening.

57.

(1) Then the Victor spoke to good Ānanda,
"Ānanda, listen now to what I shall explain:
The course of the Bodhisattva is beyond all thought,
For skill in means as well as for its wisdom.[72]

(2) "Priyaṁkara has a continuing aspiration,
That any woman who directs a look at him
With passionate intent, will lose her female form
To become a man and a truly exalted being.[73]

(3) "Ānanda, consider what good qualities it has:
Some people generate passion and are reborn in hell,
But when that passion is directed toward the heroes
It results in masculinity in heaven.[74]

[*SS* 94:3-6: *priyaṁkarasya praṇidheḥ punaḥ punar yā prekṣeta sarāgacittā/ sā bhāvaṁ parivarayitvā puruṣo bhavet yādṛgudārasattaḥ// pasyasva ānanda guṇās ya īdṛṣāḥ yenānyasattvā nirayam prajanti/ tenaiva śūreṣu janitva rāgaṁ gacchanti svargam puruṣatvam eva ca//*]

(4) "This divine male who now has done me worship,
Undertaking high awakening out of respect,
Will worship future Buddhas by the millions,[75]
And become this victor Beautiful to See.

(5) "The five hundred who have begun the path to awakening,
Will also rise to become the best of humanity;
Who would not pay respect to the World-protector,
Faith in whom produces inconceivable bliss?

(6) "Women, numbered not one or two or three,
But many hundred-thousand millions of billions,
Will attach themselves to Priyaṁkara,
And transmigrate to be reborn as men.

(7) "Who could feel aversion towards Bodhisattvas;
They are like the famous kings of healing:
Even to the defiled they are givers of well-being,
How much more to those who do them honor?"[76]

[*SS* 94:7-9: *bhaiṣajyarājeṣu mahāyaśesu ko bodhisattveṣu janayeta dveṣam/ yeṣāṁ kileśo 'pi sukhasya dāyakaḥ kiṁ vā punar yas tān satkareyāḥ//*]

58. Then Master Ānanda said to the Lord:

"Venerable Lord, it is like this. All sentient beings who stand before Sumeru, the king of mountains, have the same color—the color of gold—regardless of whether they have thoughts of hatred, serenity, or attachment, or thoughts hindered in access to the doctrine. In the same way, venerable Lord, all sentient beings who stand before Bodhisattvas, whether they have thoughts of hatred, serenity, or attachment, or thoughts hindered in access to the doctrine, all have thoughts of the same complexion—the complexion of omniscience. Venerable Lord, henceforth I will consider all bodhisattvas to be like the king of mountains.[77]

59. "Venerable Lord, it is like this. There is a great class of medicine known as Beautiful to See.[78] Any sentient being stricken by any sort of illness is healed by seeing it, whether he has thoughts of hatred or thoughts of serenity. In the same way, venerable Lord,

sentient beings who stand before Bodhisattvas, whether with thoughts of hatred or thoughts of serenity,	sentient beings who look at a Bodhisattva, whether with thoughts of hatred or thoughts of attachment,

are healed of their defilement-illnesses of desire, aversion, and bewilderment."

The Lord said to master Ānanda: "Well and good, Ānanda. What you have said is true."

Mahākāśyapa's Simile: The Wasteland and the City

60. Then the master Mahākāśyapa said to the Lord:[79]

"Venerable Lord, it is wonderful of Bodhisattva great heroes. Well-gone One, it is most wonderful! Venerable Lord: Bodhisattva great heroes abide in peaceful concentration (*praśānta-samādhi*) at the same time that they dwell in the realm of sense-desire (*kāma-dhātu*) out of sympathy for sentient beings, abiding with phenomena that are emptiness, signlessness and wishlessness and unconditioned.[80] Avoiding contact with auditor and independent-Buddha qualities, they foster great compassion and embody the thought of omniscience.

"Venerable Lord, Bodhisattva great heroes guard against all attachments. They are like this: Dwelling in skill in means that is inconceivable, they course in form, sound, smell, taste, and touch—all of which are occasions for attachment—yet are not attached to them.

"Venerable Lord, inspire me to tell a certain simile to the Bodhisattva great heroes. Well-gone One, inspire me!"

The Lord said, "Kāśyapa, be inspired."

61. Mahākāśyapa said: "Venerable Lord, suppose there were a vast wasteland, surrounded by a wall as high as the summit of existence, with several hundreds of thousands of inhabitants and but a single gate. Not far from that vast wasteland lies a great city that is prosperous and flourishing, secure and well-provisioned, populous and convivial.[81] The inhabitants of the great city do not grow old and die. The way to that great city (which is very dangerous) is but a span in width; it falls off on either side to chasms of a hundred-thousand cubits.

62. "Once, someone appears in the middle of that vast wasteland who is thoroughly learned and straightforward.

Endowed with great compassion, he is someone who seeks what would be of benefit to all sentient beings, who seeks their security, their accomplishment, their happiness, and their healing.	He is someone who seeks welfare, benefit, prosperity, and security for sentient beings.

He calls out and proclaims in the vast wasteland:

"'O friends! Not far from this vast wasteland lies a great city that is prosperous, flourishing, secure, well-provisioned, and convivial. Those who enter it do not grow old and die; and they teach measureless numbers of sentient beings doctrine by which to transcend birth, old age, illness, and death. O sentient beings, now that you know of it, come with me. Come to that great city. I will be your guide.'

63. "At that, sentient beings who are predisposed to inferiority and who aspire to self-development (*niryāṇa*) say: 'Let us seek those teachings and directions[82] without moving from here. We can develop the good qualities of being in that city while remaining here by ourselves.'

"Those sentient beings who are predisposed to greatness say, 'We will go to the city as you do.'

"Those sentient beings who are limited in merit listen to and hear his speech, but do not believe it; they do not act according to that person who is wise by nature.

64. "Then that wise by nature person departs from the vast wasteland and he sees the way: he sees the very dangerous way that is but span in width, that falls off on either side to chasms of a hundred-thousand cubits. He walls the chasms on either side with boards (*bhittī-phalaka-saṁkocana*) and crawls across the way on hands and knees. He does not look to the right or the left, nor does he look back at assailants who shout from behind and try to frighten him, but he goes his way neither anxious nor alarmed. He only has eyes for the great city,[83] and as he sees it, all his fear and his reason to fear disappears. Reaching the great city, he is freed from old age, death, and illness, and he accomplishes the welfare of measureless numbers of sentient beings, teaching doctrine to enable them to transcend birth, old age, illness, and death.

65. "Venerable Lord: Here the 'vast wasteland' stands for the wilderness of saṁsāra. The 'wall as high as the summit of existence' stands for ignorance, craving, and the false assumption of renewed existence.[84]

"The 'several hundreds of thousands of inhabitants' of the vast wasteland represent all foolish ordinary people.

"The 'single gate' in that vast wasteland is to be interpreted as the way of the single vehicle.[85]

66. "The wise by nature person represents the Bodhisattva great heroes.

"The sentient beings predisposed to inferiority who aspire to self-development and wish to seek the good qualities of the city without moving from that place, are to be interpreted as auditors and independent Buddhas.

"Those sentient beings predisposed to greatness who way, 'We will go to the city as you do' represent other Bodhisattvas great heroes.

"Those sentient beings limited in merit who listen to and hear his speech but do not believe it, stand for heterodox tīrthikas and wanderers.[86]

67. "'Departing from the vast wasteland' should be interpreted as undertaking vigorous initiatives with the thought of dedicating them to omniscience.

"The 'way that is but a span in width' represents the element of dharma (*dharma-dhātu*). The 'great chasms that fall off a hundred-thousand cubits on either side' represent the stages of the auditors and Independent Buddhas. To 'wall the chasms on either side with boards' should be understood as

the perfection of wisdom and skill in means.

vigor endowed with skill in means and the perfection of wisdom.

"To 'crawl across the way on hands and knees' corresponds to the Bodhisattva great hero winning and crossing over measureless numbers of sentient beings with the four means of attraction.

"'Assailants who shout from behind and try to frighten him' correspond to Māra and the divinities of Māra's legion who ridicule and direct sarcasm toward Bodhisattvas.[87]

"Not looking back stands for the perfection of patience and the generation of high resolve (*adhyāśaya*). Not looking to the right or left signifies his disaffection toward the stage of the auditors and independent Buddhas, and all-knowing gnosis (*sarvajña-jñāna*).

68. "The great city stands for the city of omniscience.

" 'He only has eyes for the city' stands for the Thus-Come-One, free from all fear, and for the Bodhisattva who sees the good qualities and the gnosis of Buddhahood and trains himself prodigiously in the perfection of wisdom and in skill in means.

" 'He only has eyes for the great city' stands for seeing the good qualities of Buddhahood, reflecting upon the activities and the gnosis of Buddhahood, and training oneself in the perfection of wisdom and in skill in means—and for the corresponding confidence and freedom from doubt of sentient beings.

" 'As he sees it, all his fear and reason to fear disappears': all sentient beings are confident and free from doubt.

" 'Reaching the city, he is freed from old age, death, and illness, and he accomplishes the welfare of measureless numbers of sentient beings, teaching doctrine to enable them to transcend birth, old age, illness, and death': this stands for the Thus-Come-One—the Worthy, the fully awakened Buddha.

"Venerable Lord, the Bodhisattva great heroes are endowed with gnosis. Venerable Lord, I make salutation to all Bodhisattva great heroes."

69. The Lord bestowed a "Well done!" upon master Mahākāśyapa: "Kāśyapa, well and good! Kāśyapa, with this you have created enthusiasm for the

Bodhisattva great heroes. And that is well and good. Kāśyapa, with your telling of this simile twenty million living creatures, divine and human, have generated the thought of supreme, right and full awakening. Kāśyapa, Bodhisattvas great heroes who are trained in skill in means are endowed with measureless good qualities. Kāśyapa, the Bodhisattva who is a great hero will not perform a deed that would harm himself or someone else, nor will he speak a word that would wound himself or someone else."

PART TWO

THE SKILL IN MEANS OF ŚĀKYAMUNI

Where is the Awakening in a Shaven Head?

70. The Bodhisattva great hero Jñānottara said this to the Lord: "Venerable Lord: The Lord has stated that a Bodhisattva will not speak a word that would wound himself or someone else. But Lord, why then during the promulgation of the Thus-Come-One, the Worthy, the fully awakened Buddha Kāśyapa, did the Bodhisattva, then a brahman youth named Jyotimāla who was bound by one more rebirth, say:

" 'To see a śramaṇa shave-pate? What is that to me? Where is the awakening in a śramaṇa's shaven head? Awakening is very rare.'

"Lord, what was the purpose of saying this?"[88]

71. The Lord made this answer to the Bodhisattva great hero Jñānottara: "Son of the family:

Leave off trying to assess by analysis what the course of the Tathāgatas and Bodhisattvas may be to you.	Do not try to assess the Tathāgatas and Bodhisattvas.

Why so? Son of the family: The Bodhisattvas the great heroes are endowed with inconceivable skill in means, and so these holy personages live in whatever way will serve to

bring sentient beings to maturity.	convert sentient beings.

"Nevertheless, son the family, listen will and attentively as I present an account of doctrine known as the Introduction to the Perfection of Skill in Means (*Upāyakauśalya-pāramitā-avatāraṇa-nāma-dharma-paryāya*). I will teach you something of the inconceivable skill in means demonstrated by the Bodhisattva from the time of the Thus-Come-One, the Worthy, the full and perfect Buddha Dipāṁkara.[89]

Why the Bodhisattva Continues to be Reborn

72. "Son of the family: From the time the Bodhisattva has seen the Thus-

Come-One, the Worthy, the full and perfect Buddha Dīpaṁkara, until he obtains conviction in the non-arising of phenomena, he is unerring, unboisterous, unforgetful, never faltering in concentration, unfailing in wisdom.[90]

"Son of the family: Once the Bodhisattva has obtained conviction that phenomena are unarising he may, should he so desire,

fully awaken in one week. He may fully awaken in one eon, a hundred eons, one thousand eons, or one hundred-thousand eons. On the other hand, the Bodhisattva may continue to renew his existence at will, in order to bring sentient beings to maturity. By virtue of his skill in means and his wisdom, he may fully awaken to supreme and perfect awakening whenever he pleases, or he may remain for many hundreds of eons to the future end [of saṁsāra] indefatigably.	obtain awakening in one week. He may obtain awakening after one hundred eons, in order to bring sentient beings to maturity. While continuing to renew his existence he may, by virtue of his wisdom, fully awaken whenever he pleases. On the other hand, he may remain to the future end [of saṁsāra] indefatigably.

That is the Bodhisattva's skill in means.

73. "Son of the family: the bodhisattva settles into or induces states of peaceful concentration just as the auditor does. The latter, however, becomes physically and mentally inactive, and considers that he himself has entered nirvāṇa, whereas the Bodhisattva settles into peaceful concentrations without ceasing his efforts to win over sentient beings with the four means of attraction and to bring sentient beings to maturity by means of the six perfections. And in bringing sentient beings to maturity, he generates great compassion. That also is the Bodhisattva's skill in means.

Entering the Womb

74. "Son of the family: the Bodhisattva could fully awaken to supreme, right and perfect awakening and turn the wheel of doctrine while abiding in Tuṣita heaven, if he so desired. But he thinks, 'Human beings of Jambu Continent cannot mount to the

Tuṣita abode	palace of the gods

to hear the doctrine, but gods are capable of descending to Jambu Continent.' For that reason, the Bodhisattva becomes a fully manifest Buddha on Jambu Continent. That also is the Bodhisattva's skill in means.[91]

75. "Son of the family: the Bodhisattva could become a fully manifest Buddha and turn the wheel of doctrine, if he so desired, at the very instant that he transmigrates from Tuṣita heaven, without entering the womb and coming into contact with impurity. In that case, however, some sentient beings would suspect they would doubt, they would be of two minds that he is a god, a nāga, a yakṣa, a gandharva, a magical creation, or some local spirit. With such suspicion, doubt, and uncertainty, they would not listen to doctrine in order to exhaust their defilements; they would not know doctrine, they would not undertake vigorous initiatives. For these reasons the Bodhisattva demonstrates abiding in the womb. That also is the Bodhisattva's skill in means.[92]

76. "Son of the family, do not think that the Bodhisattva enters a womb. There is no such thing as the Bodhisattva entering a womb.

How so? There is a Bodhisattva concentration called Immaculate (*vimala-nāma-samādhi*). While yet abiding in Tuṣita, the Bodhisattva settles into it, he resorts to it, and then he reaches the site of awakening from that same Tuṣita heaven without moving from that state of concentration. The gods of Tuṣita heaven think that the Bodhisattva has arisen from concentration (*samādhyas vyutthita*) changed lives (*pratisaṁdhau gata*) because they no longer see him. But the Bodhisattva great hero demonstrates all the deeds of changing lives, birth, leaving home, and austerities by means of magical creations, never moving from Tuṣita heaven. The Bodhisattva demonstrates all of these with emanations.[93] Why so? Son of the family, the Bodhisattva is clean in his habits, so he no longer enters a womb. That also is the Bodhisattva's skill in means.

77. "Why does the Bodhisattva change himself into a white bull elephant to demonstrate entry into his mother's womb?[94] The whiteness stands for innocence. How so? The Bodhisattva is the most distinguished of sentient beings; therefore he must demonstrate an entry into the womb different from that of any deity or other human being. That also is the Bodhisattva's skill in means.

78. "Why does the Bodhisattva remain in his mother's womb for ten months, rather than nine? Because some sentient beings would think, 'Aha! This infant must have faculties that are incomplete, for he has not completed his time in the womb.' To prevent such suspicions, and to show that his time in the womb and his faculties are complete, the bodhisattva stays in the womb for ten months, rather than nine.[95]

"And while the Bodhisattva stays in his mother's womb during those ten months, the gods return to see the Bodhisattva, to do him honor, and to serve him. While the Bodhisattva is dwelling in his mother's womb, they behold the Bodhisattva's enjoyment, a storied mansion arrayed with treasures that surpasses all enjoyments of the gods. Thereupon two million, four hundred-thousand divinities generate the thought of supreme, right and full awakening.[96]

"That also is the Bodhisattva's skill in means.

79. "Why does the Bodhisattva show himself to enter the womb (through his mother's right side)? Some sentient beings would think, 'The Bodhisattva is not born from his parents' embryo (*arbuda*); he is born apparitionally.' He enters the womb (through his mother's right side) in order to prevent them entertaining such a suspicion.

"Divine Mother Māyā has no wound or scar on her body after he enters, but during that period while the Bodhisattva dwells in her womb, she experiences pleasure such as she has never felt before. That also is the Bodhisattva's skill in means.[97]

Birth

80. "Why does the Bodhisattva take birth in forest seclusion, and not in town? The Bodhisattva has praised seclusion, enjoyed isolation, and lived cleanly for a long time. If he were to take birth

in town, then the gods, nāgas, and yakṣas would not come to make great (*atyanta*) offerings of divine powders, incense, flower garlands, unguents, and flowers. In addition, the human beings of Kapilavastu would become conceited (*matta*) and intoxicated (*pramatta*).	at home, then the gods, nāgas, and yakṣas would not come to make continual (*atyanta*) offerings of divine incense, powders and flowers. In addition, it delights (*pramudita*) the human beings of Kapilavastu.[98]

For these reasons the Bodhisattva takes birth in forest seclusion, and not in town.

81. "Why does the Bodhisattva's mother give birth to him inclined upon a branch of the plakṣa tree

not taking to bed (*prasavāvasthita*)?	curvaceously (*pravijṛmbhamitā-sthitā*)[99]

Some sentient beings would think, 'Divine Mother Māyā feels pain like any other woman, giving birth to the Bodhisattva.'

To show those sentient beings the ease of the childbearing and to prevent such suspicion, she gives birth to the Bodhisattva inclined upon a branch of the plakṣa tree curvaceously.

82. "Why does the Bodhisattva emerge from the womb, with mindfulness and full awareness, through his mother's right side, rather than emerging from her vagina or some other part of her body? The Bodhisattva is best in the triple world for cleanliness of habits.[100] In addition, he does so to convert sentient beings who are to be converted. Therefore, he must show his birth to be dissimilar to that of lesser sentient beings: He does not dwell in a mother's vagina—that is to say, he does not depend on, he is not born from one. That is why the Bodhisattva emerges from the womb, with mindfulness and full awareness, through his mother's right side. And after he has taken birth, there is no wound or scar on the side of divine mother Māyā. That also is the bodhisattva's skill in means.

83. "Why is the Bodhisattva swaddled by Indra, ruler of the gods (*śakro devendra*) when he has taken birth, rather than by others who are human? That is because the Bodhisattva's store of wholesomeness is blazing, bending the gods to submission, and Indra, ruler of the gods, has previously made the aspiration, 'Let me swaddle the Bodhisattva with precious clothing as soon as he takes birth.' So he is vigorous in doing great deeds of worship of the Bodhisattva.[101]

84. "Why does the Bodhisattva take seven steps unsupported when he has taken birth, rather than six or eight? The Bodhisattva takes seven steps unsupported, rather than six or eight, because

the Bodhisattva must show indubitably, as no one has previously shown, the extraordinary vigor of wonder-working power (*maharddhikabalavīrya*) and the skill (*vikrama*)[102] of a holy person;

he must show wonder-working power (*ṛddhi*) and transformation (*vikurvaṇa*) never previously shown by anyone as a holy person;

and because seven steps suffice to satisfy any sentient being, whereas six would not suffice and eight would be excessive. That also is the Bodhisattva's skill in means.

85. "Why does the Bodhisattva, when he has taken seven steps, enunciate: 'I am senior in the world. I am premier in the world. I shall put an end to birth, old age, illness, and death.'

"Son of the family: This is because Indra, Brahmā and illustrious divinities are gathered and present in that assembly. Puffed up with pride, they think that they, and not the Bodhisattva, are the highest, and they do not bow to the Bodhisattva; they fail to prostrate themselves; they make no obeisance.[103] Because they fail to bow to him, the Bodhisattva thinks, 'Indra, Brahmā, and these devaputras will be hapless, damaged, miserable, and deprived for a long time.' On that account the Bodhisattva enunciates: 'I am senior in the world. I am premier in the world. I shall put an end to birth, old age, illness, and death.'

"This universe system of a thousand million worlds resounds with the sound of that speech[104] and some devaputras who are not yet gathered there also come because of hearing the sound. And then the brahmā gods, Indra and the devaputras are alarmed; they wonder; and respectfully they cup their palms together and bow to the Bodhisattva; they prostrate themselves to him.

"For these reasons the Bodhisattva says: 'I am senior in the world. I am premier in the world. I shall put an end to birth, old age, illness, and death.' That speech of the Bodhisattva is correct, and it is also the bodhisattva's skill in means.[105]

86. "Why does the Bodhisattva give a great burst of laughter after taking birth?[106]

Son of the family, the Bodhisattva has no wild laughter, no horse-laugh generated concurrently (*saha-ja*) with desire-attachment, with aversion, or with bewilderment. Nevertheless, the Bodhisattva thinks: 'These Bodhisattvas

The Bodhisattva has no licentious laughter or frivolity. Nevertheless, the Bodhisattva thinks: 'These sentient beings

generated the thought of awakening concurrently with me. Since then I have attained awakening, but they remain stuck in dense saṁsāra because of their apathy. Alas! These sentient beings are failing to undertake vigorous initiatives in

all the factors conducive to the compassionate path to the attainment of omniscience.

"While generating great compassion in that way, he thinks: 'These sentient beings will know that the Bodhisattva has fulfilled his aspiration. They will know that they themselves have been deficient and careless. Then they will bow to me.'

"That is why the Bodhisattva gives a great burst of laughter. That also is the Bodhisattva's skill in means.

the path to omniscient liberation. If they bow to me now, they will henceforth undertake corresponding initiative towards omniscience.'

"Motivated by great compassion in that way, the Bodhisattva gives a great burst of laughter at the knowledge that both the deficient, careless sentient beings and he will have fulfilled their aspirations.

87. "Why is the Bodhisattva bathed by Indra and Brahmā when he has taken birth, whereas he is immaculate? Son of the family, this is an act of worship on the part of Indra and Brahmā.

Bathing an infant after birth is a necessary custom. The Bodhisattva must also follow

The Bodhisattva necessarily follows worldly custom. They must

worldly custom. Therefore Indra and Brahmā, seeing the necessity, bathe the bodhisattva when he has taken birth. That also is the Bodhisattva's skill in means.

bathe him as soon as they see him take birth, although the Bodhisattva is not dirty.[107]

88. "Why does the Bodhisattva return home when he has taken birth in forest seclusion, rather than proceeding to the site of awakening?

So that he might demonstrate departure from home life (to the point of renouncing sovereignty over four continents out of indifference) only after demonstrating the deed of bringing his faculties to maturation, followed by the deed of the women's quarters and the deed of pleasure and dalliance.[108] In that way, other sentient beings will imitate him in renouncing sensual pleasure, dalliance indulgence, and an extensive retinue in order to leave home for the religious life.

So that he might perform the departure from home only after demonstrating the deeds of bringing his faculties to maturation, the women's quarters, and great enjoyment and dalliance in them. Because he demonstrates renunciation of sovereignty over four continents, others will imitate him in rejecting great pleasure and dalliance in order to leave home for the religious life.

For those reasons the Bodhisattva returns home when he has taken birth in forest seclusion, rather than proceeding to the site of awakening. That also is the Bodhisattva's skill in means.

89. "Why does divine Mother Māyā expire seven days after the Bodhisattva has been born? The birth of the Bodhisattva is not at fault in this. Divine Mother Māyā expires because her span of life is exhausted, but the Bodhisattva is not at fault. While the Bodhisattva is yet residing in Tuṣita heaven, he examines the life span of divine Mother Māyā with his pure divine eye, by which he knows that no more than ten months and one week remain in the life span of divine Mother Māyā.[109] Only then does the Bodhisattva pass from Tuṣita heaven to enter his mother's womb. Therefore, son of the family, you may know by this account that divine Mother Māyā expires when her span of life is exhausted—the birth of the Bodhisattva is not at fault. That also is the Bodhisattva's skill in means.

Youth

90. "Why does the Bodhisattva educate himself in writing and engraving; in science; in mathematics and counting; in swordsmanship, archery, gymnastics, and wres-

"Why is the Bodhisattva educated in the arts? Only because it is the way of the world. The Bodhisattva needs no education

tling; in astrology; in pleasure and amusement? In accordance with the way of the world. The Bodhisattva needs no education from the outset in demonstrating (*saṁdarśana*) any art, mantra, spell, science, dance, song, instrumental music, jesting, entertainment, pleasure, or amusement that is to be found in a trichiliocosm universe: all arts and professions, both worldly and transcendent, are evident to the Bodhisattva from the moment of birth.

"Why so? Because he has been well educated in the past, and because of the generated force of the store of merit that has been brought to fruition.

from the outset in any science, song or dance, mantra or spell, weaponry, jesting, entertainment or amusement, or in any philosophic views (*darśana*) found in the trichiliocosm.[110]

91. "Why does the Bodhisattva take a wife and a retinue of male and female servants in his last lifetime? Son of the family: The Bodhisattva is not eager for sense-pleasure.

"How so? The holy person is free from desire-attachment during the time. Yet he simply must demonstrate taking a wife and a retinue of female and male servants in his last lifetime, lest some sentient beings think, 'The Bodhisattva is not a holy man, but a type of natural eunuch, and they be hapless, damaged, miserable, and deprived for a long time. To prevent doubt on the part of those sentient beings, the Bodhisattva demonstrates having a son: Rāhula. And to do this, he takes the Śākya maid Yaśodharā and the rest.[111]

92. "Some people may think that his son Rāhula is born from the embryo of his parents. Such is not the case. Why so? Rāhula has made the resolve to be his son in his last existence. Based upon that, Rāhula is conceived apparitionally, transmigrating from among the gods: he is not born from the embryo of his parents.[112]

93. "The Śākya maid Yaśodharā as well is taken because of a previous resolve.

Before the Thus-Come-One Dīpaṁkara she said: 'Brahman youth, be my husband up through your last lifetime, and I will be you wife.'

She said, 'From the time of Dīpaṁkara up through you last lifetime, I will be your wife.'

"And the Bodhisattva replied: 'Sister, I am not eager for sensual pleasure. But let it be as you intent.' Thus he promised, in return for the utpala.

"A promise made to a Buddha is unbreakable, so he takes the Śākya maid Yaśodharā.

"A promise made before a Buddha is unbreakable, so the Bodhisattva takes the Śākya maid Gopā.[113]

94. "Furthermore, the Bodhisattva simply must demonstrate having retinues of wives and servants in his last lifetime. The Śākya maid Gopā, for one, sees the Bodhisattva's triumphant body, the truimph of offerings from heaven, and the triumph of departure from home life; and she cries, 'Oh let me also come to have such qualities!' And with that high resolve, she generates the thought of supreme, right and full awakening. Accordingly, the Bodhisattva takes the Śākya maid Gopā in order to inspire her to generate a firm thought of awakening.

95. "Furthermore, some sentient beings are saturated with the business of sense-pleasure, servants, wife, work, home and property, and incapable of relinquishing their possessions for the religous life.

The Bodhisattva shows these sentient beings how to disregard craving for sense-pleasure, goods, property, and wife by taking the Śākya maid Gopā and then departing, renouncing them unconcerned for home, property, wife and retainers. Those sentient beings think: 'The youth achieved all goals (*sarvārtha-siddha*)—wife, property, retainers, and extensive goods, and then he renounced them unconcernedly in favor of the religious life. Why do we not also undertake the religious life?'

"Furthermore, some sentient beings who have the fault of sense-desire are attached to home business and incapable of renouncing it for the religious life. The Bodhisattva great hero takes a retinue for their sake.

"And they think: 'He renounced a good wife, in favor of the religious life. Why do we not also undertake the religious life (*pravrajati*)?'

96. "Furthermore, while the Bodhisattva took the Bodhisattva course in the past, he brought to maturity the wholesome qualities of some young women who did him service, and was a trusted friend to them. They made the resolve, 'May we be your wives up through you last lifetime.' Hence the Bodhisattva takes them as his retinue, in order to bring their wholesome qualities to a great fruition. Forty-two thousand women from the women's quarters he brings to the fruition of supreme, right and full awakening. The remainder he brings to a state where they are no longer subject to distress.[114]

In this way the Bodhisattva takes a retinue.	In this way the Bodhisattva does not take a retine, but

"Furthermore, some women who are afflicted by the great burning of sexual passion see the Bodhisattva and immediately find themselves to be free from passion.

97. "Furthermore, the Bodhisattva creates emanations like himself in size, color, and shape. Those creations enjoy, play and take pleasure with those women, who each think that they are playing and so forth with the Bodhisattva.[115]

But the Bodhisattva remains in a state (*sthāna*) of the enjoyment of meditative trance.	But the Bodhisattva great hero remains in the enjoyment and pleasure (*sukha*) of meditative trance and concentration.

"All of the Bodhisattva's indulgence in sense-pleasure, from the time of the Thus-Come-One, the Worthy, the right and full Buddha Dīpaṁkara, should be regarded as the same as the indulgence in sense-pleasure by those emanations.

Departure from Home

"His servant Chandaka and horse Kaṇṭhaka should also be regarded as having made a previous resolve.[116] That also is the Bodhisattva's skill in means.

98. "Why does the Bodhisattva enter trance in the shade of a jambu tree? The Bodhisattva converts seven-hundred million gods by staying there, and he shows his parents that he will leave home for the religious life. He simply must demonstrate the magnitude of his wisdom, and he must demonstrate not being left by the shade of the jambu trees; that also is the Bodhisattva's skill in means.[117]

99. "Why does the Bodhisattva go to a park whereas he is not eager for any amusements? To demonstrate old age, illness, and death. The Bodhisattva does not want to hurt his relatives,[118] but to let them know that he is to depart from home out of fear and trembling for old age, illness, and death and that he is aware that to remain at home is out of question because the home life is flawed with many disadvantages. In addition, the Bodhisattva goes to a park, although he is not eager for enjoyment and amusement, in order to show all sentient beings his fear of old age, illness, and death. That also is the Bodhisattva's skill in means.

100. "Why does the Bodhisattva depart at midnight, and not by day?[119]

To demonstrate that sentient beings should remain only where a store of merit develops into a greater store of merit. That is to say, a	To demonstrate to sentient beings that someone who wants good qualities will leave there, unquestioned,

son of the family who is eager for good qualities may already have vast well-being but he will renounce it to depart from home (at midnight, when he is unquestioned and unnoticed), and he will renounce the things he has that make for well-being so that good qualities not be allowed to diminish. That also is the Bodhisattva's skill in means.

at midnight—for if he were to remain there, his store of merit would not increase; and to demonstrate renunciaton of the things that make for well-being, and the non-renunciation of good qualities.

101. "Why are the people put to sleep by the Bodhisattva when he departs? To show that the gods are at fault—for the gods put the people to sleep. Were his relatives and the people to generate harshness and anger toward the Bodhisattva, they would be hapless, damaged, miserable, and deprived for a long time. But they believe that the Bodhisattva the great hero is not at fault, because the gods have opened the gate and carried him through the atmosphere. He puts them to sleep when he departs with the consideration that they will come to have great faith in the Bodhisattva.[120] That also is the Bodhisattva's skill in means.

102. "Why does the Bodhisattva give his horse and ornaments into the hands of Chandaka?[121] To demonstrate his contentment—

others will say that the Bodhisattva undertakes the religious life disregarding all things; he does not care for gold and silver.

and to show that the Bodhisattva does not care for gold and silver; he undertakes the religious life disregarding all things.

"Furthermore, the Bodhisattva must inspire people of the future to imitate him: 'Those who are to undertake the religious life during this promulgation should imitate me and enter the religious life based on the four usages of the nobles, disregarding all things.[122] Someone who enters the religious life seeking a livelihood has failed at the outset to enter the religious life." That also is the Bodhisattva's skill in means.

103. "Why does the bodhisattva cut his hair with a sword himself and undertake the religious life? Son of the family: no god, nāga, yakṣa, gandharva, human being, or kinnara[123] in the trichiliocosm could bear to cut his hair, for not one outshines the splendor and glory of the Bodhisattva. In addition, the Bodhisattva shows that he himself is eager for the religious life, and therefore he is someone who has faith.

"In addition, cutting his hair himself and undertaking the religious life eliminates the possibility that King Śuddhodana would

demand, out of displeasure, 'Who has dared to cut my son's hair?' Hearing that the

become angry to hear of it. Seeing that the Bodhisattva himself has

Bodhisattva himself has put his own sword to his hair, King Śuddhodana cannot say a word. That also is the Bodhisattva's skill in means."

cut his hair he cannot demand, 'Who has cut my son's hair?' He cannot execute or punish anyone."

Austerities: "Where is the Awakening in a Shaven Head?"

104. Then the Lord spoke again to the Bodhisattva Higher Knowledge: "Son of the family, listen now to why the Bodhisattva practices austerities for six years.

The Bodhisattva, being skilled in means, must necessarily alert (*udvejayitavya*) sentient beings to the functioning of their unwholesome deeds (*akuśalakarmakṛtya*), and bring them under his influence (*āvarjayitavya*).

The Bodhisattva does not practice austerities in response to obstacles brought about by past deeds (*karmāvaraṇāparādha*). The Bodhisattva, being skilled in means, must necessarily demonstrate (*uddeśayitavya*) to sentient beings the functioning of deeds.

"Son of the family: During the promulgation of the Thus-Come-One, the Worthy, the fully perfected Buddha Kāśyapa, the Bodhisattva said: "To see a śramaṇa shave-pate? What is that to me? Awakening is very rare. Where is the awakening in a śramaṇa's shaven head?'

"That speech should also be regarded as the Bodhisattva's skill in means; it should be regarded as speech with a hidden intention. The Bodhisattva practices austerities for six years by reason of that obstacle caused by a past deed.[124]

105. "With what in mind did the Bodhisattva speak those words? Son of the family: In that life, at that life, during the promulgation of the Thus-Come-One, the Worthy, the fully perfected Buddha Kāśyapa, there was a brahman youth named Jyotipāla. He had five childhood companions, sons of a well-to-do brahman clan, who had embarked upon the Bodhisattva vehicle.[125] They had forgotten the thought of awakening under the sway of an unwholesome adviser, having met an unwholesome adviser. Those five sons of the family had come to be observing brahmanical rites (*tīrthika-vrata*) instead of Buddhist rites; they were applying themselves to brahmanical mantras instead of Buddhist mantras; and they said, 'We have awakening! We are Buddhas!' claiming to be the Teacher.

"The brahman youth Jyotipāla was aware that those sons of the family were fit vessels. So being skilled in means, he wanted to gradually recover those five sons of a well-to-do brahman family from among the tīrthikas. So being skilled in means, he said to the potter Ghaṭikāra:

" 'To see a śramaṇa shave-pate? What is that to me? Awakening is very rare. Where is the awakening in a śramaṇa's shaven head?'

he said, among those tīrthikas:

"'Where is the awakening in a shaven head? Awakening is very rare. Why should I go to see him?'

"Because the youth Jyotipāla said this among the tīrthikas—'Where is the awakening in a shaven head? Awakening is very rare'—those five sons of the family were brought gradually to maturity.

106. "Son of the family, this is how it came about. At one time the brahman youth Jyotipāla was together with his five childhood companions in a certain place when the potter Ghaṭikāra arrived. The potter Ghaṭikāra spoke praise of the Thus-Come-One, the Worthy, the fully perfected Buddha Kāśyapa, and having spoken his praises, he said to the brahman youth Jyotipāla:

" 'Jyotipāla, come! Let us go before the Thus-Come-One, the Worthy, the fully perfected Buddha Kāśyapa.'

"Son of the family, then the brahman youth Jyotipāla thought: "Alas, these brahman youth are not mature in their stores of merit.[126] If I were to praise the Thus-Come-One, the Worthy, the fully perfected Buddha Kāśyapa and disparage the tīrthikas, these sons of the family would be skeptical and refuse to come before the Thus-Come-One, the Worthy, the fully perfected Buddha Kāśyapa.'

"Then the brahman youth Jyotipāla, while continuing to guard his original commitment, said

—with skill in means that is the outcome of the perfection of wisdom—

—with skill in means that is the outcome of perfection-of-wisdom gnosis—[127]

" 'To see a śramaṇa shave-pate? What is that to me? Where is the awakening in a śramaṇa's shaven head? Awakening is very rare.'

107. "How is it skill in means that is the outcome of the perfection of wisdom? The Bodhisattva coursing in the perfection of wisdom has no conception of awakening, not any conception of a Buddha.

'How is it skill in means that is the outcome of perfection-of-wisdom gnosis? The Bodhisattva coursing in the perfection of wisdom does not conceive of awakening; he has no conception of a Buddha, nor of a Buddha's gnosis.

"He does not perceive a Buddha that could be labelled 'Buddha', nor does he perceive awakening. He does not perceive bodhi inside, nor does he perceive bodhi outside; he does not perceive bodhi inside and outside. Because all phenomena are unarisen, unapprehended, awakening is entirely emptiness. So the brahman youth Jyotimāla said, with skill in means that is the outcome of the perfection of wisdom: 'To see a śramaṇa shave-pate? What is that to me? Awakening is very rare. Where is the awakening in a śramaṇa's shaven head?'

'He does not perceive a Bodhisattva; he does not perceive bodhi inside; nor does he perceive bodhi outside; he does not perceive bodhi inside and outside. Thinking, 'Awakening is entirely empty,' the youth Jyotipāla, not apprehending any phenomenon, said, with skill in means: 'Where is the awakening in a shaven head? Awakening is very rare.'

108. "Thereafter, on another occasion, the brahman youth Jyotipāla was together with his five childhood companions on the bank of a pond, when (in order that the Buddha might have the opportunity to enforce discipline upon those five sons of the family) the potter Ghaṭikāra came there to the bank of the pond.[128] He said to the brahman youth Jyotimāla:

"'Jyotimāla, come here! For lord Buddhas to arise in the world is very rare. Come to see the Thus-Come-One, the Worthy, the fully perfected Buddha Kāśyapa, to salute him, to do him honor.'

"The brahman youth Jyotimāla answered: "To see a śramaṇa shave-pate? What is that to me? Awakening is very rare. Where is the awakening in a śramaṇa's shaven head?'

"Whereas the brahman youth Jyotipāla refused to go to see the Thus-Come-One, to salute him, to do him honor, the potter Ghaṭikāra seized him by the chignon and led him to the Thus-Come-One, the Worthy, the fully perfected Buddha Kāśyapa.

109. "The five brahman youth surrounding the brahman youth Jyotimāla were influenced to come before the Thus-Come-One, the Worthy, the fully perfected Buddhas Kāśyapa.

The five youth, having no impact on the potter Ghaṭikāra, also came before the fully perfected Buddha Kāśyapa.[129]

"The five sons of the well-to-do brahman clan, who had been born into a household of wrong views, were greatly influenced. They thought: 'The potter Ghaṭikāra is risking his life to drag the brahman youth Jyotimāla by the chignon to go before the Thus-Come-One, the Worthy, the fully perfected Buddha Kāśyapa to see, to salute, and to do him honor in order to bring his wholesome qualities to fulfillment. He is to go before the Thus-Come-One, the Worthy, the fully perfected Buddha Kāśyapa. But what is a Buddha like? What are the qualities of a Buddha?'

"The five sons of a well-to-do brahman clan were influenced to go straight to the Thus-Come-One Kāśyapa to see the Thus-Come-One, the Worthy, the fully perfected Buddha Kāśyapa. As soon as they had seen the Thus-Come-One, the Worthy, the fully perfected Buddha Kāśyapa, their wholesome roots from the past were stimulated and they regained their faith.

"Finding their faith, they scolded the brahman youth Jyotipāla, saying, 'Why did you not tell us in the first place that the Teacher has such good qualities?'

110. "Son of the family: Then the five sons of the well-to-do brahman clan saw the glory and the majesty of the Thus-Come-One, the Worthy, the fully perfected Buddha Kāśyapa, and they heard his eloquence; and hearing the sound of his brahmic voice resounding, they generated the thought of supreme, right and full awakening with a high resolve.

"Son of the family: For his part, the Thus-Come-One, the Worthy, the fully perfected Buddha Kāśyapa, realizing that the sons of the family had formed a high resolve, taught a doctrinal system of the Bodhisattva collection known as the *Incantation of the Irreversible Wheels, the Diamond Word, the Nonarising of All Phenomena,*[130] which was exactly sufficient to enable them to attain conviction that phenomena are unarising.

111. "Son of the family: I therefore confirm to you, with the unobstructed gnosis of a Buddha, that if the brahman youth Jyotipāla had praised the Thus-Come-One, the Worthy, the fully perfected Buddha Kāśyapa and disparaged the tīrthikas before those five sons of the family, those sons of the family would have had no possibility or opportunity to go before the Thus-Come-One, the Worthy, the fully perfected Buddha Kāśyapa—not to mention the possibility of regaining their faith.

112. "Son of the family: That is why he the brahman youth Jyotimāla spoke those words, 'To see a śramaṇa shave-pate? What is that to me? Awakening is very rare. Where is the awakening in a śramaṇa's shaven head?'—in order to bring those five sons of the family who had entered the vehicle of Bodhisattvas to maturity with skill in means that is the outcome of the perfection of wisdom. However, son of the family, the irreversible Bodhisattva has not the shadow of a doubt in the Buddha or in awakening; nor any doubt in the qualities of the Buddha. That also is the Bodhisattva's skill in means.

113. "Son of the family: I had to bring those five Bodhisattvas to maturity, and I had to demonstrate the maturation of deeds to them. I have come to practice austerities for six years as the maturation of the *karma* of having done so. The Thus-Come-One displays such *karma* in order to demonstrate the functioning of deeds to other sentient beings who, out of ignorance, might mis-perceive righteous śramaṇas and brahmans and speak harshly of them. If they should speak thus, whether knowingly or unknowingly, with awareness or without, they would be hapless, damaged, miserable, and deprived for a long time. But the Bodhisattva has no obstacle at all resulting from the deed.

114. "Furthermore, some sentient beings speak harshly of righteous śramaṇas and brahmans and then think, 'I have lost the opportunity for liberation', persisting in their regret and failing to make further effort.

He displays that *karma* in order to dispel the regret of those sentient beings. They think, 'The Bodhisattva, when he was bound to one more birth only, during the promulgation of the Thus-Come-One, the Worthy, the fully perfected Buddha Kāśyapa said: "Awakening is very rare. Where is the awakening in a śramaṇas's shaven head?"	He spoke those words in order to dispel the doubts of those sentient beings. They think, 'The Bodhisattva great hero spoke words such as those when he was bound to one more birth only.

And he still had the opportunity for liberation. How much more so must we, who are ignorant!' So they confess their fault of evil *karma* and do not manufacture any more.[131]

115. "Furthermore, son of the family, I the Bodhisattva do austerities for six years in order to convert tīrthikas; the cause is not an obstacle from past deeds.

How so? There are śramaṇas and brahmans who eat no food but single jujube berries, sesame seeds and grains of rice, supposing that they will be purified by it. To confute them, the Bodhisattva shows that purifaction is impossible eating bad food consisting of single jujube berries, sesame seeds and grains of rice, without relying on the path of the nobles.[132]	He passes six years with śramaṇas and brahmans subsisting on individual sesame seeds, jujube berries and grains of rice, whereas purification is impossible eating bad food, without relying on the path of the nobles.

116. "For those reasons the Bodhisattva great hero says, 'Awakening is very rare. Where is the awakening in a śramaṇa's shaven head?' He practices austerities for six years with the functioning of *karma* in mind.

"During those six years of practicing austerities, the Bodhisattva causes five million, two hundred-thousand gods and heterodox ṛṣis who are devoted to wretched practices to attain the goal of realizing gnosis—

after converting them with inferior food.	and he brought them to maturity with inferior practice. Son of the family:

That also is the Bodhisattva's skill in means.[133]

At the Site of Awakening

117. "Why does the Bodhisattva go to the Awakening Tree after taking food and generating physical strength, energy, and power, rather than going while his body is emaciated and impotent? The Bodhisattva could nirvāṇize to full awakening without eating, with his body emaciated and impotent.[134] What need to mention eating inferior food? Nevertheless, the Bodhisattva takes food out of pity (*anukampā*) for people of the future

who intend to search for awakening but cannot achieve gnosis because their stores of merit are immature (*kuśalamūlapāri-pacitā)* and they worry that they will be hungry.

who, being unskilled sentient beings (*akuśala sattva*), will not search for gnosis without eating, who cannot achieve gnosis while afflicted with hunger.

"How so? Those who are comfortable can address (*abhivadanti*) the doctrine, not those who are suffering.

So I showed those sentient beings the realization of gnosis (*jñānādhigama*) in comfort. Why? Sentient beings will imitate me, saying, 'the Bodhisattva himself took food from the village girl and attained awakening with comfort of food.'

The Bodhisattva great hero (*Mahāsattva*) ate food in order to show sentient beings how to imitate him and be comfortable.

118. "Furthermore, the Bodhisattva

demonstrates the attainment of awakening

awakens

only after taking food so that the village girl Sujātā may fulfill the qualities constituting aids to awakening, and out of pity for people of the future. Nevertheless, son of the family, the Bodhisattva is capable of living without eating for many hundreds of thousands of eons on the elation and jubilation of a single trance and concentration. That also is the Bodhisattva's skill in means.[135]

119. "Why does the Bodhisattva beg for grass? Buddhas of the past enjoyed grass mats, they did not set store by cushions, so he is content with that. And the grass-cutter Svastika is enabled to fulfill the qualities constituting aids to awakening: I confirm that because he offers grass to the Bodhisattva and generates the thought of supreme, right and full awakening, he will in future time become a Thus-Come-One, a Worthy, a perfect Buddha named Viraja.[136] That also is the Bodhisattva's skill in means.

120. "After sitting down before the Awakening Tree, why does the

Bodhisattva not nirvāṇize to supreme, right and full awakening quickly, before the arrival of evil Māra? Son of the family, sinful Māra would have no opportunity to come before the Awakening Tree at all, did not the Bodhisattva create one—

did not the Bodhisattva exhort him to do so—

it would be impossible. Although there are no grounds for it, son of the family, the Bodhisattva sits before the Awakening Tree and thinks:

" 'Who is ruler of this realm of sense-desire consisting of four continents (*caturdvīpa-kāmadhātu*)?

"Who is ruler of this universe system of a thousand million worlds (*trisāhasra-mahāsāhasra-loka-dhātu*)?[137]

Under whose influence have these sentient beings come?'

"And he thinks, 'It is evil Māra. They have come under his influence.'

121. "Then the Bodhisattva thinks, 'Let me combat him evil Māra. Defeating him, I will have tamed all the realms of desire.

The many circles of Māra will be drawn in. The circle of yakṣas, the circle of demons (*rākṣasas*), the circle of gandharvas, and the circle of asuras will be drawn in, and those assembled multitudes will see the lion's play of the Bodhisattva, whereupon they will generate the thought of, and aspire to supreme, right and full awakening. For anyone else who sees, it will function as an intermediary cause for eventual nirvāṇa.'

The great circle of gods will be drawn in. The circle of Māra, the circle of yakṣas, the circle of demons, and the circle of nāgas will see the play of the Bodhisattva, whereupon they will generate the thought of awakening and find faith. Anyone who hears or sees even a little will eventually come to nirvāṇa.'[138]

122. "Son of the family: Then the Bodhisattva, seated before the Awakening Tree, emits a ray of light from the tuft of hair between his eyebrows. That light illumines this trichiliocosm, outshining the sun and the moon and eclipsing all of Māra's abodes. From the light comes a voice that says:

"'This son of the Śākyas has departed from the home of the Śākya clan. He will now nirvāṇize to full awakening, transcending the range of Māra. Countless hundred to thousands of sentient beings will also transcend his range, decreasing Māra's faction and decreasing Māra's circle. Go ahead and combat him!'[139]

123. "Son of the family:

Upon being exhorted by that light,

Upon hearing that,

Māra is torn by fierce sorrow and anguish. Angered and horrible, he loses not a moment in mobilizing and gathering his armed host of four divisions and marching to the Awakening Tree. Māra's army fills thirty-two square leagues in order to obstruct the bodhisattva.[140]

"Thereupon the Bodhisattva, stationed in great wisdom (*mahāprajñā*), great love, and great compassion, strikes the great earth with his hand like the color of gold that has developed from precious wisdom, and defeats all the legions of Māra with the strength of his love.

"Thereupon the Bodhisattva great hero (*Mahāsattva*), stationed in great love, defeats the legion of Māra with his hand that has developed from precious merit.

"No sooner has he defeated the legion of Māra than eight hundred and forty thousand millions (840,000,000) of Gods, nāgas, yakṣas, gandharvas, kinnaras, and mahoragas and kumbhāṇḍa monsters see the glory and splendor, the complexion, physique, and shape, the power, energy, and might, and the lions's play of the Bodhisattva, and generate the thought of supreme, right and full awakening. That also is the Bodhisattva's skill in means.

124. "Why does the Thus-Come-One, the Worthy, the perfect Buddha, having attained awakening, then gaze for seven days at the king of trees, not breaking his sitting position and not winking? Divinities living in the realm of form whose course is calm are present; they see the Thus-Come-One, the Worthy remain in a cross-legged position and they are vastly elated, serence, and jubilant. Being elated, serene, and jubilant, they think:

"'Let us determine upon what the śramaṇa Gautama's thought relies.'

"For seven days they investigate,

their thought concentrated (*ekotībhūta*), but they cannot discover upon what the thought of the Thus-Come-One relies.

but they cannot find a single basis (*ekasthāna*) for his thought.

Then being vastly elated, serence, and jubilant, thirty-two thousand divinities generate the thought of supreme, right and full awakening, thinking:

"'At a future day may we also, containing to course in calm, come to gaze at the Awakening Tree in that way.'

For those reasons the

Thus-Come-One

Thus-Come-Ones, the Worthies, the fully perfected Buddha,

having attained awakening, gazes for seven days at the king of trees, unmoving and unwinking. That also is the Thus-Come-One's skill in means.[141]

125. "Why does the Thus-Come-One,

the Worthy, the fully perfected Buddha, after awakening has been attained,

not teach doctrine until requested to do so by Brahmā, whereas

for an incalculable eon he has inspired and invited all sentient beings expressly to liberation?	he has inspired and invited incalculable, measureless numbers of sentient beings?

"Son of the family: At this point, the Thus-Come-One considers:

"'The worlds of gods and human beings mostly serve Brahmā and hold Brahmā to be chief. They think, "We have been created (*nirmita*) by Brahmā. We are born from Brahmā. The world has no maker besides Brahmā, no teacher besides Brahmā.' "[142]

"So at this point, the Thus-Come-One considers: 'I will make Brahmā come. I will wait for him. With Brahmā doing salutation, the worlds of gods and human beings that serve Brahmā will also do salutation to the Thus-Come-One. The Thus-Come-One will teach doctrine with Brahmā making the request, but he will not teach unrequested, lest they be uncertain as to whether accept my doctrine.'

"So Brahmā is impelled by the Thus-Come-One himself to come before him to request him to turn the wheel of the doctrine. Brahmā himself has not a single thought of making such a request of the Thus-Come-One.

126. "Accordingly, the Thus-Come-One makes Brahmā come and waits for Brahmā so that sentient beings who serve Brahmā will abandon him. At the same time the Brahmā entreats the Thus-Come-One, persuading him to turn the wheel of doctrine, some six million, eight hundred-thousand[143] Brahmās generate the thought of supreme, right and full awakening, thinking:

"'This Lord Buddha is premier among sentient beings. He is the chief. He is the very highest. Let us also come to have such gnosis and such qualities.'

"That also is the Thus-Come-One's skill in means."

PART THREE

THE TEN KARMIC CONNECTIONS

Statement of Principles

127. Then the Lord again addressed the Bodhisattva Higher Knowledge:

"Son of the family: The Thus-Come-One demonstrates ten karmic connections to sentient beings. These also should be regarded as the skill in means of the Bodhisattva and the Thus-Come-One: they also should be regarded as having a hidden meaning.[144]

128. "Son of the family: If the Bodhisattva had the slightest fraction of a hair's tip worth of unwholesomeness, he would have no opportunity to go before the Awakening Tree, the site of awakening, and there nirvāṇize to supreme, right and full awakening. There would be no occasion. It would be impossible.

"How so? Son of the family: the Thus-Come-One is endowed with all wholesome qualities; he has eliminated all unwholesome qualities that are to be eliminated. Son of the family: the Thus-Come-One has no habit-patterns at all that are yet to be eliminated—residues that would manufacture evil deeds.[145]

What need is there to mention obstacles caused by past deeds?

There is no possibility at all of a fault stemming from an obstacle caused by past deeds.

Nevertheless, the Thus-Come-One demonstrates karmic connections in order to demonstrate the maturation of deeds to certain sentient beings who waste the fruition of deeds, and to sentient beings who do not believe in karmic fruition. By showing them karmic connections in himself, the Thus-Come-One raises the question: 'If deeds come to fruition for me, the master of doctrine, why should they not come to fruition for yourselves?' He shows them the maturation of *karma*, but the Thus-Come-One himself possesses not even the slightest obstacle caused by past deeds.

129. "Son of the family: By analogy, a teacher who is already educated in letters, numbers, and engraving will recite the alphabet, in the way that

children call it out, in order to teach it to children. He is not ignorant of it, nor has he any obstacles caused by past deeds.
In any case, children hear him and imitate what they hear, reciting the alphabet in order to learn letters, numbers, engraving, and counting.

"In the same way, son of the family, the Thus-Come-One who is

already educated in all doctrine will expound it and teach *karma* in whatever ways will cause other sentient beings to purify their deeds.

already purified of karmic obstacles to all doctrine, will expound it in whatever ways will cause other sentient beings to purify their deeds. And he will teach doctrine accordingly.

130. "Son of the family: By analogy, a physician who is educated in pacifying all varieties of illness, while he is free from illness himself, will taste strong medicine in front of sentient beings who are ill—and he will praise it, he will sing its praises. The patients, seeing this, will drink the strong medicine and partake of it; whereby they will be freed from their illness.

"In the same way, son of the family, the Thus-Come-One, the great king of healing, is freed from all the varieties of illness of defilement; he has attained freedom from obstacles to all doctrine. Yet he displays *karma*, saying, 'This is the fruition of this wholesome or unwholesome deed.' He displays illness[146] thinking that sentient beings should fear and tremble at obstacles caused by past deeds and purify their deeds of body, speech, and mind.

131. "Son of the family: By analogy, soon after the son of a rich man or a householder is born, his parents may give him a wet nurse. While the wet nurse is not ill, she will measure and drink bitter and astringent medicine thinking to purify her milk for that boy.

"In the same way, son of the family, the Thus-Come-One,

the father of all the world, has no illness. Yet he displays *karma* in order to bring to maturity sentient beings who waste the working of deeds. These sentient beings are alarmed (*udvigna-mānasa*) to hear, 'Such and such a deed matures into this' and they no longer manufacture evil *karma*. That also is the Thus-Come-One's skill in means."

the father of all sentient beings, has no illness. Yet he sees sentient beings displaying the workings of *karma*, and he displays illness, saying, 'I did such and such, and this is the maturation of its *karma*.' The sentient beings hear it and obtain rebirth (*upapatti-prāpta*). Son of the family, that also should be known as skill in means."

Murder with Skill in Means: The Story of the Compassionate Ship's Captain

132. Then the Lord again addressed the Bodhisattva Jñanottara:

"Son of the family: Once upon a time, long before the Thus-Come-One, the Worthy, the fully perfected Buddha Dīpaṁkara, there were five hundred merchants who set sail on the high seas in search of wealth. Among the company was a doer of dark deeds, a doer of evil deeds, a robber well-trained in the art of weaponry, who had come on board

that very ship. to attack them.

He thought, 'I will kill all these merchants when they have achieved their aims and done what they set out to do, take all possessions and go to Jambu Continent.'

"Son of the family: Then the merchants achieved their aims and set about to depart. No sooner had they done so, than that deceitful person thought:

"'Now I will kill all these merchants, take all their possessions and go to Jambu Continent. The time has come.'

133. "At the same time, among the company on board was a captain named Great Compassionate. While Captain Great Compassionate slept on one occasion, the deities who dwelt in that ocean showed him this in a dream:

"'Among this ship's company is a person named so and so, of such and such sort of physique, of such and such garb, complexion, and shape—a robber, mischievous, a thief of others' property. He is thinking, "I will kill all these merchants, take all their possessions and go to Jambu Continent." To kill these merchants would creat formidable evil *karma* for that person. Why so? These five hundred merchants are all progressing toward supreme, right and full awakening; they are each irreversible from awakening. If he should kill these Bodhisattvas, the fault—the obstacle caused by the deed—would cause him to burn in the great hells for as long as it take each one of these Bodhisattvas to achieve supreme, right and full awakening, consecutively. Therefore, Captain, think of some skill in means to prevent this person from killing the five hundred merchants and going to the great hells because of the deed.'

134. "Son of the family: Then the captain Great Compassionate awoke. He considered what means there might be to prevent that person from killing the five hundred merchants and going to the great hells. Seven days passed

with a wind averse to sailing to Jambu Continent. without wind.

during those seven days he plunged deep into thought, not speaking to anyone.

"He thought, 'There is no means to prevent this man from slaying the merchants and going to the great hells but to kill him.'

"And he thought, 'If I were to report this to the merchants, they would kill and slay him with angry thoughts and all go to the great hells themselves.'

"And he thought, 'If I were to kill this person, I would likewise burn in the great hells for one hundred-thousand eons because of it. Yet I can bear to experience the pain of the great hells, that this person not slay these five hundred merchants and develop so much evil *karma*. I will kill this person myself.[147]

135. "Son of the family: Accordingly, the captain Great Compassionate protected those five hundred merchants and protected that person from going to the great hells by deliberately stabbing and slaying that person who was a robber with a spear, with great compassion and skill in means. And all among the company achieved their aims and each went to his own city.

136. "Son of the family. At that time, in that life I was none other than the captain Great Compassionate. Have no second thoughts or doubt on this point. The five hundred merchants on board are the five hundred Bodhisattvas who are to nirāṇize to supreme, right and full awakening in this auspicious eon.

"Son of the family: For me, saṁsāra was curtailed for one hundred-thousand eons because of that skill in means and great compassion. And the robber died to be reborn in a world of paradise.

The five hundred merchants on board are the five hundred future Buddhas of the auspicious eon.[148]

137. "Son of the family, what do you think of this? Can curtailing birth and death for one hundred-thousand eons

with that skill in means and that great compassion

with the gnosis of skill in means

be regarded as the Bodhisattva's obstacle caused by past deeds? Do not view it in that way. That should be regarded as his very skill in means.

(1) The Thorn that "Resulted"

138. "Son of the family: The Thus-Come-One initiates sentient beings into the functioning of *karma*. With skill in means, he shows an acacia thorn pierce his foot. The piercing of the foot of the Thus-Come-One by an acacia thorn should be regarded as the very power of the Buddha. How so?

The body of the Thus-Come-One, like unbreakable vajra, is indestructible.

The Thus-Come-One has a body of vajra, an indestructible body.

Nonetheless, son of the family, there are in this same great city of Śrāvastī twenty persons who are in their last lifetime and twenty persons who are enemies of those first twenty persons. The twenty persons who are enemies, each with his own dishonesty, give rise to the thought of going to the home of their particular enemy pretending to be friends and killing them. They do not say a word to each other.

139. "Son of the family: Then those twenty persons in their last lifetime and those twenty murderous persons who are their enemies come, by the power of the Buddha, to where the Thus-Come-One is—the Worthy, the fully perfected Buddha.

140. "Son of the family: Then the Thus-Come-One, the Worthy, the fully perfected Buddha, in order to bring his influence to bear upon many other people at the same time, addresses the elder, the great son of Mudgala: (Mahā-Maudgalyāyana):

"'Great son of Mudgala: Today an acacia thorn will emerge from the earth. It will pierce the sole of the right food of the Thus-Come-One.'

"Not long after Thus-Come-One has said this, a sharp thorn of acacia measuring a span in length emerges from the earth. Then the elder, the great son of Mudgala makes this request of the Thus-Come-One:

"'Lord, permit me to dispatch this acacia thorn to some other realm of the universe.'[149]

"I reply to him, 'Great son of Mudgala: You cannot dispatch this acacia thorn elsewhere from this place.'

141. "Son of the family: Then the elder, the great son of Mudgala seizes the thorn of acacia with all his might so that this trichiliocosm heaves and shakes. But that thorn of acacia does not move even a fraction of the tip of a hair.

"Son of the family: Then the Thus-Come-One by wonder-working power ascends to the heaven of the gods of the class of the Four Great Kings, and the thorn of acacia also goes to the heaven of the class of the Four Great Kings. Then the Thus-Come-One ascends to the top of Sumeru to the heaven of the gods of the Thirty-three, and the thorn of acacia also goes to the top of Sumeru. Then the Thus-Come-One ascends further, to the heavens of the gods of the Yāma, the Tuṣita, the Nirmāṇarati, and the Paranirmita-vaśavartin; he ascends further up to the world of Brahmā, and the thorn of acacia goes to the world of Brahmā as well. Then the Thus-Come-One descends from the world of Brahmā and sits on his seat, while the thorn of acacia also descends from the world of Brahmā and remains in him.

He goes likewise to the middle of the ocean, and the thorn of acacia remains in him there. Then the Thus-Come-One enters a cavern, and the thorn of acacia remains in him there. Then the Thus-Come-One sits on his seat, and the thorn of acacia remains as it was before.

142. "Son of the family: Then the Thus-Come-One grasps his right foot with his right hand. One end of the thorn of acacia sticks in the earth. He steps on the end pointed upward out of the earth. Just as the Lord steps on the acacia thorn, the trichiliocosm shakes.

143. "Then the elder Ānanda "Then the master Ānanda asks me, 'Venerable Lord: What obstacle of a deed did the Thus-Come-One previously perform of which this is the fruition?'

"I answer him: 'Ānanda, once when I had sailed off upon the ocean I stabbed and killed a dishonest merchant with a spear. This is the residue of that deed.' the fruition of that deed.'

'Then the Lord utters this stanza:

Not in the sky, not in the sea,
Not in a mountain cavern—
There is no place one can enter
To escape the effects of deeds.

(*Dharmapada* 127)

144. "Son of the family: Then those twenty people who want to kill those twenty people—the twenty people who are pretending to be friends—think this:

"'Even the Thus-Come-One, the master of doctrine, incurs a recompense of deeds. Is there any reason that we should not incur a recompense?'

"Upon that instant they disclose their offense to be an offense before the Thus-Come-One:

"'Venerable Lord, we have also been about to commit a slaughter of living beings. Before the Lord we hereby disclose our offense to be an offense, requesting the venerable Lord to accept the confessed offense as an offense.'

145. "Thereupon the Thus-Come-One teaches doctrine, beginning with

the functioning of deeds and the exhaustion of *karma*, so that those forty persons deeds, so that those forty persons realize gnosis, and thirty-two thou-

realize gnosis. Forty thousand other living creatures also realize gnosis (*jñānābhisamayante*).

sand other living creatures have their eyes opened to the dustless, immaculate doctrine (*virajavimala-dharmacakṣur viśudhyante*) and exhaust their *karma*.

For those reasons the Thus-Come-One, the Worthy, the fully perfected Buddha has a thorn of acacia stick in his foot. That also is the skill in means of the Bodhisattva and the Thus-Come-One;

it is not an obstacle caused by past deeds.

(2) Taking Forbidden Medicine

146. "Why does the Thus-Come-One snuff the

purgative *utpalahastagandha* from the king of physicians Jīvaka,

medicine of the *utpala* flower from the physician Jīvaka,

whereas he is free of illness.[150]

"Son of the family: At a time not long after the prātimokṣa rules of training have been enacted, there will be five hundred monks dwelling in a certain jungle who are in their last lifetime before release. Stricken by an illness that cannot be pacified by the remedy of foul waste, they will not seek, i.e. resort to other medicine because of their respect for the Thus-Come-One.[151]

"Son of the family, the Thus-Come-One considers:

"'What means is there for me to give them permission to seek and resort to other medicine? What way is there?'

"Why so? If the Thus-Come-One did not make other medicine permissible for them, monks of future times would not comply with the usages of the nobles; they would violate the usages of the nobles.

"'What means is there for them to seek other medicine without my giving them permission?'

"Why so? If the Thus-Come-One were to give them permission, the usages of the nobles would decline in future times.[152]

147. "Therefore the Thus-Come-One, with skill in means,

begs and requests the purgative *utpalahastagandha* from the king of physicians Jīveka.

takes the purgative of the *utpala* flower from the physician Jīvaka.

"Then the divinities of the 'Pure Abodes' class will say to those monks:[153] 'Masters, do not let yourselves die—seek another medicine.'

"The monks will say: 'Divinities: We are unable, we are helpless to supersede the rules of training established by the Thus-Come-One. We will not transgress the rules of training of the Thus-Come-One even though we may die.'

"The divinities of the 'Pure abodes' class will say to those monks: 'Masters: The Thus-Come-One himself, the master of doctrine, sought medicine other than the medicine of foul waste.

Why do you not consider seeking it? Masters:

Let you seek other medicine!'

148. "Then the monks will be freed from reluctance. They will seek and resort to another medicine and be freed from their illness. Within one week of being freed from their illness, they will actualize arhatship.

"Son of the family: Had the Thus-Come-One not sought other medicine, those monks would not seek other medicine either; they would lack any basis or opportunity to be freed from that illness, to be liberated from the defilements, and to attain Arhatship—it would be impossible. That also is the Thus-Come-One's skill in means.

(3) Empty Alms-bowl

149. "Why does the Thus-Come-One, who is endowed with all merit, return from seeking alms in a village with his bowl as clean as it was when he went?[154] Son of the family: The Thus-Come-One has no obstacles caused by past deeds at all. Nevertheless, the Thus-Come-One must pity and safeguard people of the future.

"Among mendicant monks who go to village, city, market town, metropolis, and royal capital for alms, some will be small in merit and fail to receive alms. Then they will give a thought to the Thus-Come-One:

"'The Thus-Come-One himself,

who is exalted with the majesty of all merit (*sarvapuṇya-tejasābhyudgata*), who has gathered the resource of merit (*puṇyasambhāropacita*),

returned from seeking alms in a village with his bowl as clean as it was when he went, failing to receive alms. What can we expect with our small stores of merit? Let us not be upset at failing to receive alms.'

"Considering this eventuality, the Thus-Come-One returns from seeking alms in a village with his bowl as clean as it was when he went.

150. "Furthermore, certain persons say: 'In any case, the brahmans and householders who fail to donate alms to the Thus-Come-One are possessed by evil Māra.' Son of the family: Do not view it in that way. Why so? Evil Māra is not capable of interfering with [155]the alms of[155] the Thus-Come-One.

Quite the contrary: Evil Māra inspires those brahmans and householders by the inspiration of the Thus-Come-One himself—it is not his own idea. The Thus-Come-One has no obstacle caused by past deeds at all in this regard.

He returns from seeking alms in a village with his bowl as clean as it was when he went

He demonstrates skill in means

in order to bring those same sentient beings to maturity.

"While he is fasting then, the Thus-Come-One as well as the community of monks (*bhikṣu-saṁgha*) have no unhappiness.

"While the Thus-Come-One is fasting then, Māra and the gods of Māra's class, and other gods as well, decide to assay whether the śramaṇa Gautama or his auditors are not unhappy. They examine the thoughts of the Thus-Come-One and the community of auditors (*śrāvakasaṁgha*). Day and night they examine the thoughts of the Thus-Come-One and community of auditors, but they cannot see a single state of mind that is unhappy.

They are just as they were before: neither haughty, not downcast.[156]

151. "Upon the instant, seventy thousand divinities find faith and bow to the Thus-Come-One. And the Thus-Come-One teaches all of them the precise *dharma* that will make their *dharma* eyes pure, dustless, and immaculate in regard to *dharmas*.

"As for the brahmans and householders: they will at some other time hear of the qualities and the contentment of the Lord Teacher, and they will gather before the Lord. They will disclose their fault to be a fault and the Thus-Come-One in his turn will reveal to them an account of the four truths of the nobles. Thereupon twenty-two thousand living beings among the generations of gods and human beings will have dharma eyes that are pure, dustless, and immaculate in regard to *dharmas*.

"For these reasons the Thus-Come-One returns from seeking alms in the well-to-do brahman village with his bowl as clean as it was when he went.[157] That also is the Thus-Come-One's skill in means;

it should not be understood as an obstacle caused by past deeds.

(4) Cañcā's Feigned Pregnancy

152. Why does the brahman girl Cañcā bind a wooden bowl to her belly and cast aspersions upon the Thus-Come-One, saying: 'Śramaṇa, you have made me pregnant. Now keep me with food and clothing'?

"Son of the family: The Thus-Come-One has no obstacle caused by past deeds. The Thus-Come-One might fling away the brahman girl Cañcā to the distance of as many realms of the universe as the Ganges' sands. But the Thus-Come-One is deliberately impassive; he displays the functioning of *karma* out of skill in means.[158]

"How so? In future, during this promulgation, it will happen that monastics are caluminated. They will be filled with regret and disheartened; they will be disaffected and in danger of failing. When aspersions are cast upon them, they will recollect the Thus-Come-One and say:

"'The Thus-Come-One, who is endowed with all wholesome qualities, was himself subject to calumny. Why should we not be?'

"And they will immediately overcome the aspersions and practice celibacy that is perfectly pure and highly refined, not allowing it to fail.

153. "Assuredly, the brahman girl Cañcā is permeated by evil *karma* and abundantly unfaithful. Obscured by such obscuration caused by past deeds, there is no question but that she wounds this promulgation with here actual aggregates, elements, and sense-fields, and is permeated by evil *karma*. To caluminate the Thus-Come-One even in a dream would contaminate one's waking life.

"Son of the family. If the Thus-Come-One had any means by which to stop her from the manufacture of unwholesome *karma*, he would stop her. If the Thus-Come-One could act to protect her, he would protect her.

"The girl Cañcā, permeated by evil *karma*, will go to hell as soon as she dies—as one would for caluminating the Thus-Come-One even in a dream. Assuredly, if the Thus-Come-One knew how to protect her, he would protect her.

Why so? The Thus-Come-One will not abandon any sentient being. That also is the Thus-Come-One's skill in means.

(5) Death of the Wanderer Sundarikā

154. "Why is the Thus-Come-One, who is all-knowing, impassive to the wanderer Sundarikā, slain by fellow wanderers and thrown in a dump in the Jeta Grove? The Thus-Come-One knew what is occurring, for he is endowed with gnostic vision without obstruction to omniscience (*sarvajñāpratihata-jñānadarśana*).

unobstructed gnosis (*apratihata-jñāna*).

The Thus-Come-One could certainly exercise magical power of a sort [159]that would prevent the sword from penetrating the wanderer Sundarikā, and fling her elsewhere.[159]

But the wanderer Sundarikā's span of life is exhausted, and it is certain that she will die by violence at the hands of others.

"And because of that incident the other tīrthikas are quite confuted by their own misdeed, knowing that whatever will result in fostering wholesome qualities and developing stores of merit for sentient beings is what the gnosis of the Buddha is grounded on, in whatever way it should be grounded (*sthāpita*).

But the Thus-Come-One knows that the wanderer Sundarikā must certainly die, because her span of life is exhausted.

"And he knows that because of the incident the other tīrthikas will be quite confuted by their own misdeed. Whatever will result in fostering wholesome qualities is an exercise of magical power (*adhisthāna*) by the Thus-Come-One—and that is the gnosis of the Buddha.

155. "The Thus-Come-One does not enter the city for one week. During that period he converts six-hundred million gods. When the week has passed, the four assemblies gather before the Lord,[160] and the Lord teaches doctrine in ways that enable eighty-four thousand living beings

to give rise to gnostic vision.

to discover gnosis.

That also is the Thus-Come-One's skill in means.

(6) Eating Horse-feed

156. "Why does the Thus-Come-One together with the monastic community, during a rainy-season retreat in the Vairambha district, when he eats food, for three months put people at ease and eat barley horse-feed of the brahman Vairambha?

"Son of the family: The Thus-Come-One is aware that the householder[161] will request his presence and that of the monastic community and then fail to appreciate him. Yet he deliberately accedes and makes himself impassive.

157. "Why so? The Thus-Come-One, together with the monastic community, spends three months eating barley that is the feed of five hundred specific horses. All of those five hundred horses are progressing in the Bodhisattva vehicle. They have each done service to a victor of the past, and they have done evil deeds and manufactured evil *karma* under the influence of an unwholesome adviser, because of which *karma* they have been reborn in the animal world. Among those five hundred horses is one horse who is a thoroughbred. He is known as the Bodhisattva Sūryagarbha (Core of the Sun). He has been reborn intentionally, by virtue of a resolve. Bodhisattva Sūryagarbha has previously, when they were human beings prompted all those five hundred horses to undertake awakening; now he is reborn there in order to bring them to freedom and maturity. Impelled by that thoroughbred horse, all the five hundred horses have come to recollect their previous lives and to evince the thought of awakening.

158. "Son of the family: That is why the Thus-Come-One accedes,[162] out of sympathy with those five hundred Bodhisattvas-become-horses—for the sake of those who have been reborn in the animal world. Each of the five hundred horses offers half his barley-feed to the five hundred monks there. The thoroughbred horse offers half his barley-feed to the Thus-Come-One. The thoroughbred horse eats half his food himself and with a horse's neigh prompts all the five hundred horses to confess their misdeeds and make salutation to the monastic community headed by the Buddha, making them understand that half of the barley-feed of each is to be eaten by the Thus-Come-One and the monastic community. So those five hundred horses confess their misdeeds and generate faith in the monastic community headed by the Buddha.

159. "Those three months pass and eventually the five hundred horses all pass on to be reborn among the gods of Tuṣita. And having become gods, they offer food, pay respect, venerate, show honor to, and worship the Thus-Come-One, and the Thus-Come-One teaches them doctrine that will assure them of supreme, right and full awakening.

"The one groom who has tamed and tended the five hundred horses is confirmed by the Thus-Come-One to become the independent Buddha Taming the Mind (*Sudāntacitta).

"The Thus-Come-One further confirms that the thoroughbred horse will make offerings to measureless numbers of lord Buddhas, fulfilling the qualities that are aids to awakening, and then appear in the world as the Thus-Come-One, the Worthy, the perfected Buddha Taming the Mind.

160. "Son of the family: For all that, there is no human food unpalatable to the Thus-Come-One. Son of the family, just suppose that he the Thus-Come-One should ingest even wood, clumps of earth, pebbles, and bricks: there would be no more excellent taste, nor better savor in this trichiliocosm than that wood, clumps of earth, pebbles, and bricks. Why so? Son of the family: Because he the Thus-Come-One is endowed with the most excellent taste as a mark of the superman;[163] therefore any unpalatable food, as soon as it is eaten, becomes in the body of the Thus-Come-One endowed with taste surpassing that of food of the gods. Son of the family, you should therefore know by this incident that all the food of the Thus-Come-One is palatable.

161. "Son of the family:

At that time, the monk Ānanda thinks unhappily;	The elder Ānanda thinks in pity:

"'The Thus-Come-One has renounced the sovereignty of a universal monarch for the religious life. Now he is apparently eating barley horse-feed.'

"The Thus-Come-One divines his thought and says: 'Ānanda, do you know the taste of this?' handing him a barley corn. He marvels to eat it, and says to me:

"'Lord, I was born and raised in a king's palace, yet Lord I have never before been granted the experience of such an excellent taste.'

By virtue of being given it,

the monk	the master

Ānanda is happy and healthy eating nothing else for a week.[164]

162. "Son of the family: By this incident you should understand that the Thus-Come-One is skilled in means, whereas he has no obstacle from past deeds whatsoever. Furthermore, son of the family, this display of a karmic connection serves as a lesson in doing what one has promised to do, for sentient beings who issue invitations to righteous śramaṇas and brahmans but distractedly fail to show them honor.

"Son of the family, note the character of the Thus-Come-One:[165] Anyone requesting the presence of the Thus-Come-One is confirmed by the Thus-Come-One to be not liable to fall into the states of woe (*avinipāta-dharmin*), although he fails to show him honor.

163. "Son of the family: Furthermore, among the five hundred monks who accede to the three-month rainy-season retreat together with the Thus-Come-One, who eat barley horse-feed with him, there are forty monks who course in desire-attachment and course in pretty features. If they were to eat palatable food during that period, their preoccupation with desire-attachment would increase drastically. As it turns out, by eating bad food their obsession with desire-attachment is attenuated and disappears. They dispel their obsession with desire-attachment and they all attain arhatship within one week subsequent to those three months.[166]

"Son of the family: That is why the Thus-Come-One, out of skill in means, eats barley horse-feed for three months—in order to influence those five hundred monks and to bring those Bodhisattvas to maturity. This is not the fault of an obstacle from a past deed; it also is the Thus-Come-One's skill in means.

(7) Backache

164. "Why does the Thus-Come-One while observing Uposatha day declare: 'Kāśyapa, my back is unwell. You explain the limbs of awakening'?[167]

"Son of the family: At that time, eight thousand divinities have been drawn into that assembly,

converted by the auditors. established in the vehicle of the auditors.

The monk Kāśyapa has already prompted them again and again to generate faith in the Buddha, the Doctrine, and the Community, and in the duty to act with vigilance; and they have already heard him tell of the limbs of awakening. That being the case, they would not take note of doctrine taught by anyone but the monk Kāśyapa—not even if it were taught by a hundred-thousand Buddhas. So the monk Kāśyapa explains the divisions of the limbs of awakening in detail, and those eight thousand divinities realize gnosis.

165. "Furthermore, sentient beings who do not come to hear doctrine because they are impaired by illness and in bad health, sentient beings who do not study doctrine because they have no opportunity to hear it will then think:

"'The Thus-Come-One himself, the master of doctrine, was freed from his illness by hearing an account of the limbs of awakening. Why should we not listen to doctrine?'

166. "Son of the family: That is why the Thus-Come-One says: 'Kāśyapa, my back is unwell. You explain the limbs of awakening'—in order to influence those divinities, and to display respect for the doctrine to sentient beings who are ill. But it is not the case that the body of the Thus-Come-One has illness. Why so? Son of the family: The Thus-Come-Ones, the Worthies, the fully perfected Buddhas are Dharma-bodies, they do not have gross bodies composed of the elements.[168] That also is the Thus-Come-One's skill in means,

and not an obstacle caused by a past deed.

(8) Headache

167. "Why does the Thus-Come-One, when the Śākyas are destroyed, say: 'Ānanda, my head aches; I my unwell'?

"Son of the family: Certain sentient beings are not aware that the Thus-Come-One has ended his relatives' aggregate of suffering

up to the peak of existence (*bhāvagra*). that is beginningless (*anādi*).

When this occurs, they think:

"'Since the Thus-Come-One left home for the benefit of the world, the dynasty has perished. Far from defending his relatives, the Thus-Come-One does not wish benefit for his relatives, nor does he wish their welfare nor their well-being; he does not wish their survival and happiness.'

"To guard against such thoughts on the part of those sentient beings, the Thus-Come-One says to the elder Ānanda: 'Ānanda, my head aches; I am unwell.'[169]

168. "Son of the family: At the time that the Thus-Come-One says to the elder Ānanda, 'Ānanda, my head aches; I am unwell,' three thousand annihilationist divinities and very many murderous sentient beings have been drawn in. The Thus-Come-One displays a karmic connection, saying that his head aches and he is unwell as the residue of a murder, in order to initiate those annihilationist divinities and murderous sentient beings to the functioning of deeds (*karma-kāraṇa*). the course of *karma* (*karma-patha*).[170]

"In displaying that deed of speech, the Thus-Come-One converts ten thousand living beings among the generations of gods and men. That also is the Thus-Come-One's skill in means,

and not an obstacle caused by a past deed.

(9) Scolding by Bharadvāja

169. "Why does the Thus-Come-One acquiesce to the insults of the brahman Bharadvāja, who scolds him with five hundred forms of abuse?[171]

"Son of the family: The Thus-Come-One could take the insulting Bharadvāja and return his insults, or fling him to some other place, or render him by the exercise of magical power unable to utter a single word of abuse to the Thus-Come-One. However, many gods and human beings have been drawn into that assembly. They see the absence of discouragement or arrogance in the Thus-Come-One, his composed and benevolent disposition, his mind

firm, yet

gentle and tender; and they see him generate the power of forbearance, remaining the same as he has been before. Then four thousand living beings generate the thought of supreme, right and full awakening. With that goal in mind the Thus-Come-One makes himself impassive to the insults of the brahman Bharadvāja

—but the Thus-Come-One has no obstacle caused by past deeds in any form.

And with that, the insulting brahman Bharadvāja finds faith in the Thus-Come-One; he then takes refuge in the Buddha and creates the seeds for attaining nirvāṇa. That also is the Thus-Come-One's skill in means,

and not an obstacle caused by a past deed.

(10) Persecution by Devadatta

170. "Son of the family: That is why the Bodhisattva

great hero

is pursued by Devadatta from life to life and rebirth to rebirth: that also is the Bodhisattva's skill in means.

"How so? I fulfilled the six perfections and accomplished the welfare of numberless sentient beings dependent upon Devadatta. By What account? Son of the family: Whether sentient beings were well-off but ignorant of giving and receiving, then Devadatta would approach the Bodhisattva and beg for his children, wife, and sovereignty, his hands, feet, and eyes, his head and such things that are difficult to give and that create

well-being (*kuśala*) a store of merit (*kuśalamūla*)

for sentient beings. Undiscouraged, the Bodhisattva would give these things, and numberless sentient beings would see this and be gladdened, inspired, and jubilant; energetically they would devote themselves to giving and aspire to awakening, thinking, 'Let us be the same way.'[172]

171. "Furthermore, Devadatta and countless sentient beings who wish to violate ethics would see the Bodhisattva refuse to violate ethics and then hold to ethics themselves. While imitating the Bodhisattva, the sentient beings would see his triumphant forbearance. Then when they were insulted, reproached, or struck, they would not be irritated but would themselves fulfill forbearance. In that way also he accomplished the welfare of sentient beings.

172. "Occasions upon which Devadatta dispatches assassins, incites the elephant Dhanapāla, and inspires

the hurling of a rock the raising of a catapult

to kill the Thus-Come-One, should also be regarded as the Thus-Come-One's skill in means, rather than the fault of obstacles caused by past deeds.[173] Why so? Dependent upon that skill in means, he accomplishes the welfare of numberless sentient beings.

173. "Son of the family: To summarize, Devadatta the ambitious is my teacher.[174] All ten karmic connections should be regarded as the Thus-Come-One's skill in means, rather than as the faults of obstacles caused by past deeds. How so? Sentient beings who waste the functioning of deeds and their maturation are introduced to the functioning and the maturation of deeds: the Thus-Come-One displays a karmic connection with skill in means to indicate that such and such is the maturation of such and such a deed. And hearing it,

sentient beings can no longer be passive in the face of obstacles caused by unwholesome deeds, and the need to manufacture wholesome *karma*.

they are benefited.

INSTRUCTIONS ON TRANSMISSION OF THE SŪTRA

174. "Son of the family: This explanation of the teaching of skill in means is to be kept secret. Do not speak of it, teach it, explain it or recite it in the presence of inferior sentient beings whose store of merit is small.

"Why so? This teaching is not the stage of the auditors and independent Buddhas—what need to mention

foolish common persons who are inclined to something inferior (*hīnādhimukta-bālaprathagjana*)?

sentient beings whose store of merit is small (*hīnakuśalamūlasattva*)?

"Why so? They are untrained in this skill in means. Why so? They have no need for it. No one but a Bodhisattva great hero is a fit vessel for this teaching of skill in means; no one else is to be trained in this teaching.

175. "Son of the family: By analogy, in the darkest gloom of the night an oil lamp is lit, and all the household vessels are illumined. In the same way, son of the family, if a Bodhisattva hears

and believes

this teaching of skill in means,

all sentient beings will see the Bodhisattva undertaking his practice and they will think: "He will educate them in skill in means (and sentient beings who are unprepared will have it only in name).

he will see all the practices of a Buddha and will train sentient beings in them as well.

"Son of the family, adhere to this and fathom it. The son or daughter of the family who is eager for awakening will travel a hundred-thousand leagues when it comes to his ears that this perfection of skill in means will be taught somewhere. Why so? Hearing that teaching on skill in means, the Bodhisattva will attain illumination and be freed of doubt and hesitation in regard to the qualities of the Buddha."[175]

176. Then all among the four assemblies of the world, including the gods, who were fit vessels for this system of doctrine, who had been drawn into that assembly, heard this system of doctrine promulgated by the Lord. All who had been drawn into that assembly who were not fit vessels, did not have it this system of doctrine enter their ears.

While this system of doctrine was being presented, seventy-two thousand living beings generated the thought of supreme, right and full awakening.

177. Then master Ānanda asked the Lord: "Venerable Lord, what is the title of this system of doctrine? How should it be remembered?"

The Lord answered: "Ānanda, remember this account of doctrine as the *Teaching of the Perfection of Skill in Means.*

Remember it as the *Chapter on Skill in Means.* Remember it as the *Teaching on Skill in Means, the Great Secret of All Buddhas.*"

Remember it as the *Select Chapter of the Skill in Means of All Buddhas.*"

OVATION

178. Thus spoke the Lord. Enraptured, the master Ānanda as well as the Bodhisattva great hero Jñānottara, those of the vehicles of the auditors and the independent Buddhas as well as householder men and women progressing in the vehicle of the Bodhisattvas, and the world including gods, human beings, asuras, and gandharavas, acclaimed the Lord's promulgation.

Thus spoke the Lord enraptured; and Ānanda, the Bodhisattva great hero Jñānottara, and the world including gods, human beings, asuras, and gandharvas, acclaimed the Lord's promulgation.[176]

COLOPHONS

Indian Colophon

From the noble, the great Ratnakūṭa doctrine system of a hundred thousand chapters, Chapter Thirty-eight—the Great Secret of

The Skill in Means Mahāyāna-sūtra is completed.

All Buddhas, the Skill in Means, the Question of Bodhisattva Jñānottara—is completed.

Tibetan Colophon

Translated and edited by the Indian preceptors (upādhyāya) Dānaśīla and Karmavarman in collaboration with the editor-translator, the *bande* ye-shes-sde, and subsequently revised in accordance with the "new language" enactment and published.[177]

1230 *ślokas.*

600 *ślokas*; 2 rolls.

NOTES TO THE TRANSLATIONS

1. Title, Fa-ch'eng Version: "The noble Mahāyāna scripture entitled 'Skill in Means' (*Ārya-Upāyakauśalya-nāma-mahāyānasūtra*)".

Title, Ratnakūṭa Version: "From the noble, the great Ratnakūṭa doctrinal system of a hundred thousand chapters, Chapter Thirty-eight: The noble Mahāyāna scripture entitled 'The Chapter of the Great Secret of All Buddhas, the Skill in Means, the Question of Bodhisattva Jñānottara' (*Ārya-Sarvabuddhamahārahasya-Upāyakauśalya-Jñānottarabodhisattvaparipṛcchā-parivarta-nāma-mahāyānasūtra*)."

2. Śrāvastī was capital of Kośala under King Prasenajit; there the Buddha passed twenty-five of the forty-five rainy seasons of his teaching career (*Mpps* 1:173 n.3). One among his residences there was the park purchased by the merchant Anāthapiṇḍada from Prince Jeta for the number of gold pieces required to cover its surface (reference *ibid.* 181 n.2).

On the numbers of monks and Bodhisattvas see Introduction, section 1, p. 4 above, and the discussion at *Mpps* 1:233-34. The Lord emerged "at a later time" (R) than the preceding Sutra in R.

"Yet in training" and "adepts" (*śaikṣa, aśaikṣa*): the latter state is equivalent to Arhatship; see *Ak* 45b.

All the Bodhisattvas (according to R) are "great heroes" (*mahāsattva*): Bodhisattvas of a high stage who cannot regress (*Mpps* 1:309-15, *Hob.* 141).

"Well known for supernatural knowledge" (*abhijñā-abhijñāta*): wonder-working power, divine ear, divine eye, knowledge of others' thoughts, and recollection of past lives (*Mpps* 1:328-33).

"Mastered the incantations" (*dhāraṇī-pratilabdha*): spells drawn from passages of scripture (*ibid.* 317-31).

"Eloquence. . .": *asaṅga-pratibhāna.*

"Calling forth suprnatural knowledge": *abhijñā-nirhāra.*

"Conviction that phenomena are unarising" (*anutpattika-dharmakṣānti*): a stage of understanding that precedes gnosis, *jñāna*; *ibid.* 1:325-27, 2:902-26; see sections 49, 72 following.

3. Sanskrit, references for this formula at Rawlinson 1977:13 and 28 n.107. Inclusion of "bodhisattva great heroes" follows *Mv*; the *Śūramgamasamādhi* has "Bodhisattvas". *PWA* and *Lotus* have "all sentient beings" (*sattva*)—as Rawlinson observes, clearly the earlier version.

4. R: "[he] can give single morsel of food to all sentient beings."

5. "Omniscience" (*sarvajñatā*)=Boddhahood; he dedicates the merit gained by the deed (the "store of merit", literally "wholesome root", *kuśala-mūla*) to the attainment of Buddhahood by others.

Vimalakīrti fills an assembly with a morsel of food; see Lamotte 1976:212-13, discussion *ibid.* 311.

Giving is the premier meritorious act, and dedication of merit the highest form of giving, so *PWRg* ch. 31, discussed Introduction, section 5 above; see also *Mpps* 2:721, 723. On Buddhist versus Vedic "transference of merit" see Ogubenine 1982.

6. R: "he dedicates it to".

7. So *PWRg* 31:15-17: Sentient beings might donate countless gifts, etc., to Buddhas, Arhats, and Pratyekabuddhas, but with an inferior religious aspiration; the Bodhisattva, etc., who appreciates (Conze: "rejoices at", *anumodayi*) their merit, and

dedicates (Conze: "turns over") the merit of his appreciation to their full awakening, surpasses the merit of their generosity.

R Ch glosses "recipients" as auditors and independent Buddhas.

8. "Morality etc." comprises the set of five "spiritual aggregates" (*dharma-skandha*) that more or less replace the five "grasping aggregates" (*upādāna-skandha*) that constitute the ordinary person: matter, sensation, ideation, karmic formation, and consciousness. ("More or less": see the discussion at *Ak* 1:27). The spiritual aggregates are part of the thirty-seven aids to awakening (*bodhipakṣya, PWP* 671); they are also attributes of the adept (ref. *CPD* s.v. *asekha*) and of the Buddha (*Mhv* 103-8). See also E s.v. *skandha* (3).

9. Fa "considers and appreciates"; the original may be *saṁgṛhītam anomodate.*

R Tib reverses the order of "well-being" and "suffering" in this section, disturbing the flow of the argument.

10. The meaning "expose" for *āviṣkaroti* is clear at *Upāli* 25; see also *ākoṭita* at *SS* 40:21, cited E s.v. *ākoṭayati.*

11. Fa reads "one element, one morality. . ." For this passage see Harrison 1992, n. 81.

This last set comprises the three trainings (Fa), or the five spiritual aggregates (R).

"Element" or "realm" of dharma (*dharma-dhātu*): the cause of all the attributes of the nobles (*ārya-dharma*). See Vasubandhu, *Madhyāntavibhāga-bhāṣya* cited Ruegg 1969:97; Asanga, *Abhidharma-samuccaya* cited *ibid.* 107; and *Kp* 80: "auditors evolve from the element of dharma". Cp. usage at section 67 following.

12. The Bodhisattva does not discount, i.e. underestimate, himself (*ātmano 'paribhavanatayā*): *Bbh* at Tatz 1968:118.

13. Rarely would a Bodhisattva be impoverished, because of his store of merit. "At least to some extent" : See CPD S.V. *antamaso.*

14. "Measureless" thus applied to the thought of awakening seems to support Fa's reading of the previous sentence, rather than the implication of R that the gift itself is measureless. Strictly speaking, it is the merit of a gift given with a high mind that is measureless.

15. The principle being expounded is that generosity gives rise to future well-being, and especially to wealth.

"Marks of a superman" (*mahāpuruṣa-lakṣaṇa*): thirty-two physical characteristics of someone destined to temporal or spiritual greatness (a Cakravartin or a Buddha). "Excellent taste" appears also at section 160 following; ref. noted there.

"Jewel in hand" (*ratnapāṇi;* or *ratnahasta*, attested *Mv* 1:141:13 as the name of a former Buddha): probably to be identified with the wish-granting jewel of a Cakravartin; in later sūtras the name of a Bodhisattva (*Lotus* p.2, *Upāli* 11; cp. *Mhv* 655, other ref. E s.v. *ratnapāṇi*); on the personification of Buddha-epithets see Snellgrove 1957:64; on the cakravartin-buddha-jewel complex see Senart 1882:44. At *Mmk* 425:19 Ratnapāṇi is listed among Bodhisattva between Kṣitigarbha and Maitreya, which may indicate his identification with Śākyamuni.

16. R Tib is here corrupt: (1) By harmonization with other texts (e.g. *PWA* 269), (Fa) "accomplishes" (*abhisaṃskaroti*) becomes (R) "outshines", "surpasses" (*abhibhavati*). (2) R Ch and Fa name the three sorts of meritorious work (*puṇyakriyāvastu*). Cp. *PW A* 124 on appreciation versus other meritorious woks. (3) By internal harmonization, R Tib continues with "come to achieve....." as above (not translated).

17. R Tib interpolates here: "those of the auditors" vehicle and those of the vehicle

of Independent Buddhas". This was perhaps an interlinear comment intended to indicate that the Bodhisattva does not dislike individual colleagues, but their attitudes.

18. The reasoning: To become a Buddha, one must take the Bodhisattva path, so "Buddhas evolve from bodhisattvas"; to become an arhat (whether *śrāvaka* or *pratyekabuddha*), one must hear the teachings of a Buddha, so they "evolve from Buddhas".

"I am foremost. . ." echoes the words of Śākyamuni as he enters his last existence; see section 85 following. Fa "I alone am foremost" is probably a misreading.

The following section (no. 15) is absent from R Ch as well as from Fa; it is again (cp. n. 17 above) a later qualification to his dislike for auditors.

19. On the mutual inclusiveness of the six perfections, see *Bhadramāyā* 121, *Mpps* 2:750-69 and 750 n. For example, on giving see *ibid.* 752-54: Failing to give, one will be reborn poor, one will steal, etc.; immorality thus arises from not giving. To give to someone who is poor, on the other hand, decreases the likelihood that he will steal, etc., thus fostering morality.

20. He gives a warm welcome and energetic service even if the beneficiaries lack good manners and lick their hands and bowls—a practice of some heterodox schools that are forbidden by the monastic code (*Mhv* 8587, E s.v. *avalihaka*, PTSD s.v. *apalekhana*. Fa seems to miss the point, as does R Ch.

21. Fa (or Dharmarakṣa) seems to have misconstrued, taking *saumanasya* "happy" for *āśvāsa* "breathing" or "refreshed", and *avikṣepa* "free from wandering" for *agrahaṇa* "not grasping". All the terms found in R represent experiences in meditative trance (*dhyāna*); they are also used by Kumārajīva in this context (*Mpps* 2:763).

22. Ordinary giving, not dedicated to the attainment of Buddhahood, brings the karmic reward of a good rebirth; it binds one still to saṃsāra.

23. The remainder of this line up to "Son of the family. . ." is lost in R Tib by homioarchton; it is attested by R Ch.

24. "Aggregates..." (*skandha-dhātv-āyatana*): a circumlocution made to avoid implying the presence of a unitary "self". The sense is, "Let me not enter nirvāṇa with this organism—in this lifetime." Final clause absent in Skt.

25. Each of the four seminal transgressions (*mūlāpatti*) or defeats requires expulsion from the monastic community: uncelibacy, murder, theft, and false claim to spiritual attainments. See *Mhv* 8363, Prebish 1975:50-53.

26. T Tib omits.

27. In this context, *prātimokṣa* refers not to rules codified for the monastic community (as at Prebish 1975), but to simplicity of lifestyle, to equanimity, and to restraint. For ascetic practices permitted by Buddhaghosa see VM 2.

28. R omits. Skt omits "Bodhisattva", reading "so long as a son of the family fails to confess. . ."

29. A monastic who is defeated (see n. 25 above) is "defrocked" for life, and it is popularly believed that he cannot win the goal during that lifetime. (Technically speaking, however, that is not the case. See Dharmamitra, *Vinayasūtra-ṭīkā* O 5622 cited Tsong-kha-pa, Tatz 1986:197-98.) In the same way, to adopt lesser-vehicle concerns, and thereby relinquish the greater-vehicle goal of reaching Buddhahood for the sake of all sentient beings, is to violate the most fundamental element of the Bodhisattva moral code and consequently cease to be a Bodhisattva. On the other hand, such defeat does not last for a lifetime in the case of a Bodhisattva; like the less serious monastic offenses, it can remedied by confession and reform.

30. The term of address "master" (*āyuṣman*) is but modestly respectful. The Buddha discouraged its use within the community; in later usage it signifies a monastic of junior standing (*Bbh* commentaries at Tatz 1986:147 and n. 188. See also the article by J. May, *Hob* 380-92, and n. 149 below.

On the role of Ānanda see Introduction, section 2 above. Fa shows Nanda, half-brother to the Buddha, but Ānanda is attested by a parallel passage of the *SS* (section 57 following). For an instance in the Ratnakūṭa where the Tibetan reads Nanda and the Chinese reads Ānanda, see Lalou 1927:237-38.

31. "Dissembling" or "concealment" (*pratichādana*) is a factor needed for a deed to become a defeat (see *Ak* 4:39cd, p. 99); but Ānanda is overzealous in presuming that failure to inform on his fellow would constitute a transgression. In cases of "indeterminate" (*aniyata*) intimacy, evidence is to be brought by "a trustworthy laywoman" (Prebish 1975:62-64).

32. King at the Head of the Masses: **gaṇapramukharāja*. Fa or Dharmarakṣa is apparently trying to render *gaṇaprabhārāja*: King of Much Light.

"Inside a certain house": R reads "in a certain other city"—certainly, an error by internal harmonization.

R's interpolation "in six ways" may by an instance of harmonization with other scripture, e.g. *Mv* 2:10:9 etc.; *Suv* Tib 160:7-8, Eng 89; *PWA* 293. The earthquake here is ironical: the premier earthquake of Buddhist literature occurs when the Buddha relinquishes his will to live, deciding to enter nirvāṇa three months later—an event for which some traditions blame Ānanda (see Frauwallner 1956:156-62, Bareau 1963:2:71-76). The earth also quakes at the nirvāṇa of Ānanda (*Aśokāvadāna* 339).

33. "Seven times the height of a palm tree" is correct; Fa has the same at section 38 following (see also *Mv* 1:334:14, etc.) The ability to levitate is not a standard set by *vinaya*, but a part of older yogic lore; see O'Flaherty 1973:378 ref. motif no. 25e, "sex destroys *tapas*".

34. "The [Buddha] present before us" points to the doctrine of multiple Buddhas, an issue among the schools; see *Mpps* 1:299-308.

35. Ānanda is exaggerating the *vinaya* formula for confession; see e.g. E s.v. *atyaya*, CPD s.v. *accaya*.

36. A person. . .absolutely peerless (*aprati[sama]pudgala*): as opposed to a bodhisattva.

"Meditative calm" (*śamatha*): as opposed to skill in means.

To "exhaust the outflows" (*āsrava-kṣaya*) is to eliminate desire-attachment, aversion, and ignorance.

37. The five faculties (*indriya*) of a Buddha are faith, vigor, mindfulness, concentration, and wisdom; they are opposed in the earlier literature to the moral laxity of indulgence in the five objects of sense-desire (*pañcakāmaguṇa*).

38. But R Ch agrees with Fa: *anuśaya*.

39. R Tib omits.

40. "Spiritual exercise": literally, "dharma door" (*dharma-mukha*). Matter is composed of four elements: earth, water, fire and air. In this discursive meditation, the earthy (i.e. solid) components of the (female, etc.) body are conceived as being the same as earth (soil, etc.); the aim is avoidance of lust. See *VM* 11:31, 41; 18:19.

41. "For the welfare of": R Tib "as medicine for".

42. "'Incalculable' eon" (*asaṁkhyeya-kalpa*): according to the secondary sources

(*Ak, Bbh*, etc.), one "great" (*mahā*) eon contains twenty "intermediate" (*antara*) or ordinary eons (Lamotte 1976:184n.; cp. Bu-ston 1:119-21, ref. E s.v. *asaṁkhyeya*). That the sūtra intends a particular number of years, is doubtful.

"Free from obsession" (*niḥparyutthāna*): free from manifest defilement. "Buddha-field" (*kṣetra*)": When he becomes a Buddha, the world in which he resides becomes a pure land, free from defilement; see Lamotte 1976, Appendix note 1.

43. "Store of merit" (*kuśala-mūla*): at its last occurrence, Skt has only "merit", "wholesomeness" (*kuśala*). Fa adds a phrase: "(relinquish) or diminish".

44. The phrase "I know this for myself" (*abhijānāmi*) points to the knowledge (*abhijñā*) of past lives.

Jyotis is a brahman youth (*māṇavaka*). R elevates the woman from water-carrier to merchant's daughter—inadvisably, for the lower her caste, the more dramatic the effect of his cohabitation with her. In the tale of the Bodhisattva as Megha alluded to at section 93 following, Yaśodharā is a water-carrier.

Surāṣṭra is a tentative reconstruction. There Nārada—the Bodhisattva in a past life—also fails in morality; see *Jātaka* tr. 3:277.

45. R "maiden" here et. seq. In Fa, "son of the family" might refer to Jyotis.

46. Fa: "Let this woman, who was about to die, be happy." "Seven steps" may allude to the Indian ceremony of marriage; cp. also notes to sections 49, 51 following; also *Jātaka* 352v: enemies will not ordinarily approach within seven steps.

47. "Four stations of Brahma" (*brahma-vihāra*): love, compassion, appreciation, and evenmindedness. Success in the (meditative) cultivation of these four brings rebirth as a brahma god, despite Jyotis' previous uncelibate conduct, *abrahmacarya*. See section 35 following. See also the study of the *brahma-vihāra* in Wiltshire 1980.

48. "Second thoughts..." (R): an ending for jātaka narrative after *Lv*, etc.; references E s.v. *vimati*. For the wife of Śākyamuni, R has "the Śākya maid Gopā"; see section 91 and note following.

Jyotis' deed of mixed *karma*—lust and compassion—brings about the moderately positive result of rebirth on a high plane and temporary release from the process of saṁsāra; cp. sections 136-37 and note following. R has mistranslated *itvareṇa* (or has read *itareṇa*), thereby reading "a little" instead of "transitory" passion.

49. Text emended from *paścānmukham*, an error of internal harmonization (cp. Skt cited sections 33 above), to accord with Tib. The reading has occasioned uncertainty; see *SS* tr. Bendall 163, E 388b. The correct reading may also be *sahasrāṇi saṁsārāt parāṅmukhani'bhūt*, as at *Suv* Tib 60:4-5, Eng 31:2-3.

50. On Kokālika see *Mpps* 1:63n., 2:806-13. The incident to which this passage refers is described best by Chinese sources. During the rainy season, Śāriputra and Maudgalyāyana pass a night in a potter's house in which a woman, unknown to them, is hidden. She dreams and has an impure discharge. Kokālika passes by the next morning, notices the discharge and the two monks inside, and proclaims them to be impure, finally coming before the Buddha. Unlike Ānanda in the incident above, he refuses to recant. (Thus he is guilty of suspension offense no. 9; see Prebish 1975:56.) The next night he dies and falls into hell.

The traditional accounts do not regard S. and M. as being at fault for failing to prove their innocence to K. In one version (*ibid.* 813n.), M. descends into hell to try to save him. On K., see also Caillat 1984 : 64-65.

M. can fly according to tradition; see e.g. *Theragāthā* 104 and references.

51. Fa Kakutsunda, R Krakucchanda (Tib *log par dad sel*; so correct *Mhv* 90, E 196a). The two refer to the same Buddha, most often numbered the third of the six preceding Śākyamuni; cp. *Mv* 1:1-2. The Tib version of *Vk* apparently reports a tradition in which the two differ; see Lamotte 1976:266-67. The *Sgra-sbyor* (15-16) explains the two Tib translations as deriving from these originals: (1) "destroyer of saṁsāra" *karma-kuṁsaya* and (2) "dispelling misguided beliefs" *kutsida-(chanda)-atikrānta.*

52. "Physically": they would have fallen directly into hell without waiting to be reborn there. The ṛṣis may have erred by assuming the rainfall to be caused by uncelibacy; see *Jātaka* no. 526 (vol. 5), O'Flaherty 1973:42-52.

53. Maitreya, the Buddha to come after Śākyamuni, resides in Tuṣita heaven. See Lamotte 1958:775-78, 197n.; *Mv* 1:51:5-7.

54. "Beyond the range" also at *Upāli* 16. All acts of the high-stage Bodhisattva are accompanied by gnosis (*jñāna*), unlike those of the auditor, etc. Gavāṁpati, for example, re-chewed his food—as though it were a cud—even after attaining arhatship; "such an act is not accompanied by gnosis" (*Mpps* 3:1659).

55. The sixty-four arts form part of *kāma-śāstra*; see *Kāmasūtra* 3: song, instrumental music, painting, self-adornment, etc. *SS* mentions this analogy (94:9-11): *upāyakauśalyasūtre ca gaṇikāvat kṛtarthe bodhisattvo nirapekṣas taṃ sattvaṃ tyajati.* But this, adds Śāntideva, is practice of someone at the level of the six perfections, not of someone who has attained the stages.

56. R expands the "three doors to deliverance" (*vimokṣa-dvāra*) by adding "selflessness" from the list of the "three marks of all conditioned things"; see Conze 1962:34-36, 59-69. Cp. the contamination at sections 44, 60 following.

To paraphrase: The Bodhisattva may indulge himself in sensual pleasures that would normally lead to a lower rebirth, if he has first purified them of defilement by comprehending their emptiness, etc. Cp. *Kp* 48: "Poison cannot kill someone in possession of mantras and medicine, so. . . the poison of defilement cannot send a Bodhisattva to a distressing rebirth when he possesses gnosis and skill in means."

For the non-generation of defilement likened to a burnt seed, see commentaries to *Yogasūtra* 2:2 cited by Potter in O'Flaherty 1980:246.

The term *varṇa* in this context suggests the later usage of *gotra* "class" in the sense of "inherent qualities of Buddhahood"; see Ruegg 1969 passim.

57. Bendall (*SS* tr. 161) takes *prabhujya*, not unreasonably, as "having enjoyed"; so "whatever he wishes, by a single thought of omniscience based on the strength of knowledge after having enjoyed all the kinds of desire, he is born in Brahma's world."

Cp. the elaboration at *PWA* 233-35. See also Galloway 1988:146.

58. "Warrior" is literally "archery teacher"; see *CPD* s.v. *issācāriya.* Fa: "teacher of arrow and weapons."

59. "Living in a state of carelessness (*pramāda-vihārin*): a designation for the secular life, see references to Saṁyutta Nikāya, etc. at *CPD* s.v. *appamāda.* On Māra, ruler of the realms of sense-desire, see section 120 and note following.

60. The sense is clear, but the originals diverage, perhaps Fa *darśanīyānvaya-ghoṣanimittān,* R *anuvyañjānakṛitighoṣavarṇanimittān.*

The name Priyaṁkara is attested by the *SS*; Śrī Dakṣiṇottarā includes the reconstruction of effaced letters (ed. Vaidya 94:2, ed. Bendall 168:4, tr. 164). The English rendering "Superior Donations" follows Ch and Tib as analogous to the name

Jñānottara, but it might also be taken as a *dvamdva*: "Lower and Higher", or "Lucky-Unlucky".

61. For a similar analysis see *VM* 15:15-16, also 18:31: "The psycho-physical organism is empty, inert." "Rigid" is literally "seventh level" (?*saptapada*); cp. parallel passages at *Dbh* 1:RR *jaḍa, PWA* cited pp 381:5 *astambhitatā*. See also *Ak* 6:34ab, especially p. 203: the Streamwinner, who is to be reborn only seven times, resembles a man bitten by a venomous serpent who will die after walking seven steps (*saptapada*).

62. The heaven of the Thirty-three (*trāyastriṁśa*) at the peak of Mount Sumeru is inhabited by the vedic equivalents of the gods of Mount Olympus; for a description see Tatz 1977:98-99. The seven precious substances according to Lotus Skt are gold, silver, beryl, coral, pearl and crystal (Hurvitz 1976:183, 373); other lists E s.v.

On sex change Mahāyāna sūtras see Paul 1979.

63. Fa: "I have obtained immeasurable wonder-working power (*ṛddhi*)." The Skt is undoubtedly *ṛddha*, "opulence"; R Ch makes the same error as Fa.

64. Cp. *Mv* 3:311-12: A poor woman offers a rag robe to the Bodhisattva as an ascetic, is reborn in Trāyastriṁśa and wonders what her reward would have been if he had made use of robe. Cp. also the story of the village cow-girl Sujātā, who according to *Mv* gives Śākyamuni food because of her lust for him, and is predicted as a consequence to Independent Buddhahood (*Mv* 2:206:17-8).

65. Both versions are unclear. The original term seems to have been *suvarṇāvabhāsa*, read by Fa as *varṇāpramāṇa* and mistranslated by R Tib as *shin tu 'phags pa*.

66. R Tib: "seven times."

67. Fa applies "wholesome" to "maturation", which may be preferable.

68. So Fa, translating *udārodārena* "vast and sublime"; R translates *dharmodārena* "with the best offerings of doctrine".

69. R Tib "thinks of me",

70. "Devil lore" *kākhorda* generally applies to women, according to Burrow (1935:780-81) s.v. *khakhorna*. Had Dakṣiṇottarā attempted to seduce a Śaivite ascetic, she might well have been cursed to sweat to death; see O'Flaherty 1973, motif no. 11c, 36a.

71. R "showing respect (*ādara*)"; Fa "taking refuge (*śaraṇa*)"—the act of conversion—is preferable.

72. Fa: "the mental course of a Bodhisattva is inconceivable,/ For the wisdom of its skill in means."

73. R Tib: "and quickly become a confident (*vaiśāradya*) male". R Ch seems to read *ādara* for *udāra*.

74. R Tib has the "heroes" going to heaven.

75. Fa "for millions of eons."

76. Fa/Dharmarakṣa reads *kileśo* as an ablative, so: "Even from defilement they make a gift of well-being." This may accord better with the comment that follows in *SS* (94:9): Where benefit for a sentient being is at issue, a "transgression" of desire-attachment is no transgression.

Bhaiṣajyarāja is later considered a specific Bodhisattva, but the sense here is: No one hates a successful physician. In the chapter of the *Lotus* devoted to that Bodhisattva, it is said that a woman who studies the chapter will be reborn as a male in Sukhāvatī. See also Birnbaum 1979:24-25, *EB* 2:4:669, *Mpps* 1:17n.1 and references, *Hob* 228.

77. Mount Sumeru, in the cosmology of the *Ak*, has sides of gold, silver, lapis and crystal. Anything stationed before the side of gold is tinged a golden color by the sun's reflected light. (The southern side is lapis, hence our sky is blue.) Ref.Tatz 1977:36 and n. 44.

For the same *upāya* by which the Bodhisattva reflects the thoughts of others, see *Bhadramāyā* 110; as done by the Buddha see *ibid.* 15. Alternatively, hateful thoughts and the like are obstacles of study; see *PWA* 167-68.

78. This "king of healing" is also mentioned in the *Gaṇḍavyūha*; references E *sudarśana* 10. The passage of the *Up* has been noticed by Birnbaum 1979:24-25.

79. This Kāśyapa, called "great" to distinguish him from others, is known for solitude and austere practice (*Mpps* 2:1547, Lamotte 1976 s.v. Mahākāśyapa, E s.v. Kāśyapa). He is associated at an early stage with the New Wisdom school, especially by the *Kp*.

80. R again contaminates the three marks of all conditioned things with a forth item; cp. sections 43, 44 above.

81. This list of adjectives, plus others from this tale, are found at *Mhv* 6413-19; but neither Fa nor R corresponds to it precisely. R Tib adds here (by dittography): "the great city has but a single gate."

82. "Those directions (*pradeśa*)" is a pun of "region" upon "teachings".

83. Here the adjective "great" disappears in R and crops up in Fa.

84. "False assumption of renewed existence": *bhava-dṛṣṭi*. Cp. *PWA* (tr. Conze): "assumption of a self, a being, a living soul, a person, of becoming (*bhava-dṛṣṭi*), of not-becoming, of annihilation, of eternity, of individuality, etc." But R reads "ignorance of craving for renewed existence (*bhava-tṛṣṇā*), interpreting the latter as one among the three cravings (for sense-pleasure, renewed existence and annihilation; see E s.v. *tṛṣṇā*, from *Ak*).

85. "Single vehicle" is *eka-yāna* (*Mhv* 6418, from this text). More than in *PWA* (e.g. 248, translated "same vehicle"), its usage here approaches that of the *Lotus* and other later sūtras; see *Vk* tr. Lamotte 1976:163-66 and n., Hurvitz 1975, Ruegg and Kunst in Lancaster 1977. The sense is that there is, ultimately, only one vehicle—those of the auditors, etc., being merely provisional.

86. *Tīrthikas* and *parivrājikas*: brahmanical and non-brahmanical religieux; see the incidents at sections 152 and 154 following.

87. On Māra see section 120 following. The four means of attraction (*saṁgrahavastu*) are giving, kind words, helpfulness, and consistency of words and deeds.

88. The incident will be treated at sections 104-16 following. Śramaṇas are non-brahmanical religieux, including Buddhists. For (the Buddha) Kāśyapa, R Tib has a variant Dīpaṁkara.

89. Dīpaṁkara is the first Buddha of the Auspicious Eon; references n. 51 above. In his presence the Bodhisattva begins the path to Buddhahood by generating the thought of awakening. That rebirth is again adduced at section 93 following; see *Mv* 1:1:14-2:1.

90. "Conviction...": see n. 2 above. "Unerring" etc. are three (R: five) of the eight "special qualities of a Buddha" (*āveṇika-buddhadharma*) known to *Mv* (1:160:8ff), Pali commentaries, and later sources (*CPD*, E s.v.; full listing at *PWP* 159-60). Number 4 is slightly misquoted here.

What stage is this in the Bodhisattva's career? The "special qualities of a Buddha" here precede "conviction", which is in the Mahāyāna a Bodhisattva attainment. "Conviction" may be taken to correspond to the point in the *Nk* account (134) at which the Bodhisattva, as the Cakravartin Vinitāvin under Buddha Kauṇḍinya, masters the tripiṭaka, the three higher forms of knowledge, etc. *Mv* ignores these attainments in its chapter on Vijitāvin (vol. 3), because it has already assigned the Buddha-qualities to a Bodhisattva of the eighth stage; all its past-life stories of the Buddha go back only as far as the eighth stage, at which point he has acquired the qualities of a Buddha (*Mv* 1:105-7).

PWA refers to "conviction" as characteristic of an irreversible (*avaivartika*) Bodhisattva who is certain to achieve the next step, gnosis (241, translated "cognition"). *Dbh* likewise places "conviction" at the seventh stage, adding that nirvāṇa has been achieved at Stage Six; the Bodhisattva then declines to enter cessation but renews his exertions at Stage Seven (7 K-L). For other references see E s.v. *anutpattika*; also *EB* 1:179-80, *Dbh* Eng 218 n. 22.

91. Tuṣita is a heaven of middle level, and thus ideal for the penultimate rebirth; other advantages are discussed at *Mpps* 1:267-68. On Tuṣita and Jambu Continent as cosmology see Tatz 1977:36-40. In a famous passage, Vimalakīrti connects human beings and gods by ladders (Lamotte 1976:246).

92. Cp. *Mpps* 1:21: "If the Bodhisattva could walk and speak from birth, people would say, '...he must be a god, a nāga, or an asura. How can we follow his teachings?" On the misapprehension by some early disciples that he is a god, etc., see *ibid.* (from Aṅguttara 2:38, etc.)

"God" is *deva*; the Skt *nāga* is a serpent deity of water; *yakṣa* is a demigod; *gandharva* is a celestial musician. See Tatz 1977:78-79.

"For these reasons": literally, "for these causes and conditions (*hetupratyaya*); cp. *Mv* e.g. 1:153:7.

93. "Reaches the site of awakening" (*bodhimaṇḍa-niṣīdana*): a reference to the Awakening Tree; see sections 177ff following. "Magical creation", "emanation"; on *nirmāṇa-kāya* see *Mpps* 1:20 n. and references.

His birth is like the birth of gods, according to *Lv* 47, v. 22. In accounts older than *Up* he descends in person, but "mindful and in full awareness" (as he emerges from the womb at section 82 following; see Majjhima 3:118 cited Thomas 1949:30-31, *Mv* 2:9:20). In some versions, he is attended by the gods of Tuṣita. (So also *Nk*; the 1880 translation is preferable to the revision of 1925; cp. 1880:62, 1925:149. Further references are to the 1880 edition.)

94. This elephant does not appear in the earliest accounts, See *Nk, Mv, Lv* ibid. n. 93 above: he enters her side in the form of a white elephant while Mother Māyā dreams of the event. See also Thomas 1949:34; Senart 1883:353-57 on elephants in pre-Buddhist literature.

95. The sūtras specify ten (lunar) months exactly—not a bit more or less as with other gestations (Bareau 1974:205; see also *Nk* 65, Thomas 1949:153, *Mv* 1:148:1, *Mpps* 1:271 noting at 269 that he has the strength of Nārāyaṇa, the Indian Hercules). See also Foucher 1949:40 on the *Lv* account.

Bareau shows that the sūtra accounts of a Bodhisattva's last nativity do not mention Śākyamuni; they deal with a past Buddha or with Bodhisattvas in general (1974:203).

96. This interpolation by R of a storied castle (*kūṭāgara*) comes from *Lv* (49:15-16; other ref. E s.v. *paribhoga*), with a variant: R *samatikrama* "surpasses" for *Lv*

kāmāvacarana "all the mansions of the plane of sense-desire appear in it". The earliest simile is that he resembles a jewel while in the womb, untouched by its impurities; his mother is like a casket shrine; the gods pay their respects (the four deities that guard the world, Mahārājika); see Bareau 1974:204, Majjhima 3:118, *Nk* 65, *Mv* 1:144 and 2:16-18; Senart discusses it 1882:261-62.

The number of deities is two *niyutas* and four hundred-thousand in R; at *Lv* 54:8 it is thirty-six *nayutas* of deities and human beings.

97. R understands this passage to deal with the emergence from the womb rather than entry into it—perhaps to justify its interpolation in the previous section (but the emergence proper occurs at section 82 following), or perhaps because the "right side" motif belongs originally to the emergence (see Bareau 1974:203). Sources prior to *Up* Fa do not stipulate that he enters through here right side, but *Lv* does (43:6).

Here the magical (*nirmita*) birth of the bodhisattva—as specified at section 76 above—is distinguished from the apparitional (*anupapāduka*), non-sexual birth of hell-beings, gods and ghosts; see *Mpps* 1:270-71, *Ak* 3:8cd. In the *Mv* they are not thus distinguished (1:177:13, cited Introduction n. 34 above; see also *Mv* 2:20:16-17: his mother's side is not rent because "Buddhas manifest themselves with physical bodies made by mind"). On her lack of wounds in the sūtras see Bareau 1974:206; also *Lv* 69:17. On her lack of discomfort see *Nk* 65; Majjhima tr. Thomas 1949:30; *Mv* 1:147:17, 2:12-15. The phrase "physical and mental joy" in R Ch is closest to *Lv* (43:16-17). On the birth of the Bodhisattva see also Hara 1980.

The generatrix is referred to as Māyādevī. In the vinaya sources taken to be earliest, only male progenitors and relatives are named (Bareau 1962:8ff). "Divine" or "queen" Māyā appears at Digha Nikaya 17, etc. (Ñanamoli 1972:183). For pre-Buddhist use of the word *māyā* see Senart 1882:270ff.

98. Fa is preferable on this last point; the famous pride of the Śākyas is not out of place at the nativity, nor is delight: see its usage by Aśvaghoṣa at *Bc* 1:58-59. *Nk* records a festival with intoxicants, garlands, and perfumes at the time of the conception (63-64). See also Thomas 1949:31; and the confusion of conception with birth-date in *Lv*, cited *ibid.* 34.

99. Fa is supported by *Mv, Lv* and artistic representations. So also early sūtras (Bareau 1974:206; Bareau notes the resemblance of her posture to depictions of sylvan yakṣiṇī). In specifying the plakṣa tree (ficus infectoria, the "waved-leaf fig"), *Up* follows *Mv* verse (1:149:15-16, 2:19:17-18) agreed with by *Lv* prose (61:17-18). *Mv* prose (2:18:8-9) and *Nk* (66) name the śāla tree (shorea robusta); so also *Mv* 1:220:8-9 for the birth of the Buddha Dīpaṁkara. See also Thomas 1949:33-34, Foucher 1949:43 and n., Senart 1882:240-41. At *Bc* 1:8, Māyā is encouched.

100. "Cleanliness of habits" (*śuci-samācāra*) refers primarily, of course, to celibacy. The triple world consists of the realms of sense-desire, attenuated materiality and non-materiality; see Tatz 1977:33-36.

Most early accounts likewise emphasize the cleanliness of the birth; see Bareau 1974:206. He emerges through the right side also at *Mv* 1:148:1-2, 1:220:10-11; *Lv* 61:20-22; *Bc* 1:11. A note to *Bc* 1:9-10 identifies previous heroes of Indian mythology who are born from "some other part" of the body.

101. Early sūtras: The four gods take and swaddle him so he will not fall to the ground (Bareau 1974:206). *Nk* (66-67) engages almost all deities save Indra. See also Nanamoli 1972:4, Thomas 1927:33. *Bc* has no formal reception. *Mv* does not name the

gods; but the world-protectors bear him "on the hip" (2:21:5-6). *Lv* 61:23-35: Indra and Brahmā swaddle him with clothing; so also *Mpps* 3:1343. But cp. section 87 following.

For Indra's prior service see for example *Nk* 67.

102. Or "stride". The question is posed in these words at *Mv* 2:21:1-2, save that *Mv* has *apariśrānti* "not tired (of the womb)", whereas *Up* and *Lv* (62:13) have *aparigṛhīta* "unsupported". The "seven steps" motif is found in early sūtras (Bareau 1974:207). At *Mv* 2:20:19-22:7, 24:5=1:219:3 on Dīpaṁkara, and at *Bc* 1:14 he takes seven steps upon the earth and gazes into the directions. At *Lv* 62:13, Majjhima 3:123, etc. he takes seven steps in each directions. Texts, other references *Mpps* 1:6-10n.

See the discussion by Mus at 1933:879-980, especially 887-95 on seven steps and the seven planetary bodies. Cp. Przyluski and Lamotte 1932:169 on the early conception of the *bhūmis* as seven planetary bodies. See also Foucher 1949:50-52.

See also Mus 1933:822-30 comparing the nativity to the brahmanical consecration (*abhiṣeka*) of a king, and inspecting the cardinal points to demonstrating sovereignty over the world. For mythic parallels to non-Indian cultures and the "solar" thesis see Senart 1882, ch. 2, esp. 241ff.

103. Disrespect by the brahma gods is not of course indicated in the oldest accounts; no reason is given for the seven steps, but most versions take the opportunity to expatiate upon his eminence (Bareau 1974:208). Indra, furthermore, does not belong among the proud, for he has done the swaddling recounted just above. On the brahma gods see Tatz 1977:34, 107. Cp. *Mv* 2:22:2-5: he laughs, and makes his enunciation is response to the māra gods, who have suggested that he become a secular monarch. *Lv* adds, "This is my final rebirth". Texts, ref. *Mpps* 1:6-10n.

104. The addition by R follows *Lv* 62:24-25. "Thousand million worlds", or trichiliocosm. On a single Mount Sumeru world-system see Tatz 1977:36-40. On a thousand million of them see *Mpps* 1:447-49; Lamotte 1976, Appendix n. 1.

105. Cp. *Mv* 2:22:6-7 (and variant 1:220:5-6): "The teachers praise this as a karmic reward,/ For thus the teaching of the Buddhas is announced. *Lv* 62:25: "This is the way of the Bodhisattva's higher knowledge, created as a karmic reward."

106. Earlier occurrences only *Mv* 2:20:20 and 1:218:18 (on Dīpaṁkara): *mahāhāsaṁ ca ūhati*. In *Mpps* (1:6) the laugh becomes a "lion's roar", descriptive of his claims in the preceding section. Discussion Mus 1933:815-16.

107. R Ch attests this last clause. In early sūtras, two clouds pour water and gods assist the bathing; see Bareau 1974:206-7, Nanamoli 1972:5; also *Nk* 66-67 cited Thomas 1949:33, in which his inherent cleanliness from afterbirth is also noted. So also *Bc* 1:16. In some early sources and at *Mv* 2:23:4-7, 24:16-20, *Sbhv* 1:45:17, the showers are hot and cold. *Lv* 62:1: *bodhisattvaṁ snāpayataḥ sma*; here the bath servants are two nāga kings. See discussion of ritual ablution at Foucher 1949:49-50.

108. "Sovereignty over four continents (*caturdvīpa*): the mantle of a Cakravartin, who reigns over the four continents of human beings in a Mount Sumeru world-system; see Tatz 1977:37, 94-95.

"Women's quarters (*antaḥpura*): the arts of pleasure—dance, song, women, etc. are implied; see *Lv* ch. 13, Foucher 1949:87-88, *Up* section 90 following.

109. The same question and answer are found at *Mv* 2:3:1-20 (and 1:199:3-19, in context of Dīpaṁkara). The interpolation by R of "*pure* divine eye" resembles *Mv*: "he examines his mother with great mindfulness obtained by pure karma." *Lv* (70:25-29) poses the question in the same words and answers (but without referring to a prior

examination) with two reasons: her span of life is exhausted, and his later departure from home, if she lived to see it, would "break his mother's heart". *Nk* (65) reasons that the womb that housed the Bodhisattva is a virtual caitya, and cannot be later inhabited by someone else (cp. *Mv* 2:3:15-16).

Early sūtras mention her death (Nanamoli 1972:4), and Bareau (1974:208-9) speculates on development of the motif. In most versions she goes to Trāytriṁśas; in Pali sources she goes to Tuṣita, but then in Pali sources she is later found at Trāyatriṁśas when the Buddha visits her. On the pre-examination see Foucher 1949:32-35, *Nk* 60-62, *Sbhv* 36-39, *Mpps* 1:268-69.

110. Weaponry and sport are the crux of this stage of his life—which is, essentially, his betrothal. The oldest sources lack incidents connected with the betrothal, as discussed by Bareau, who places development of the legend of his youth at the mid-second century B.C. (1974:262). At *Nk* 76 the Bodhisattva tells his father that there is no art he need learn; yet he must demonstrate to his clansmen that he is not entirely pleasure-loving, but is also prepared for the eventuality of war (see also Thomas 1949:48). In the *Nk* he shows it with archery. In the *Mv* (2:74:8-75:19) he demonstrates warfare and pugilistics (*yuddha, niyuddha*) in order to win his bride, but only archery is described. This is done in response to a complaint by her father that he has been raised in the women's quarters and has no education in the arts, archery, elephantship, weaponry, or political science (*Mv* 2:73:6-9). The Bodhisattva proposes a seven-day tournament in any or all of the arts, archery, warfare and pugilistics, cutting and stabbing, foot racing, wrestling, elephantship, horsemanship, chariot, bowmanship, swordsmanship and reasoning.

In *Lv* the reason for the demonstration is the same, though the names of the bride and her father differ. He has not shown any skill in the martial arts. (The previous chapter, no. 10, contains the schoolroom incident in which he excels his teacher in letters and numbers; see also Senart 1882:294.) He engages in a tourney of letters, numbers, sports, and martial arts (*Lv* 102:7ff), concluding with an account of the sixty-four arts (108:8-18). The second list in R is drawn from that list of sixty-four. Only mantras and spells (*mantra-vidyā*) are not found there; they may derive from a misunderstanding of an alternative tradition, e.g. *Bc* 2:24: he learns "all the fields of knowledge (*vidyā*) suitable to his class; *Bc* 2:35: he does not learn harmful *vidyā*, but pacific knowledge *jñāna*; and 2:52: he studies peaceful *śāstra* and renounces arms.

See also *Mv* 1:153:4-5: the Bodhisattva knows all arts without a teacher. On epic parallels in winning brides see Foucher 1949:84-85; Senart 1882:299-304, comparing the Bodhisattva to Rāma and Kṛṣṇa.

111. The question in *Mv* (1:153:6-8) goes: "Bodhisattvas, from the Tuṣita existence forward, do not indulge in sense-pleasure. . . How then in Rāhula born?" The question is posed also in the *Śūraṁgama-samādhi* sūtra (139, 177-78, discussed Pye 1978:196). The Bodhisattva's harem is established by his father even before the marriage; see sūtra description of the three palaces at Nanamoli 1972:8-9, Thomas 1949:47; also *Nk* 75-76; the expansion at *Mv* 2:48:3-5, 115ff; the single palace at *Bc* 2:28-32.

For the name Rāhula, Fa has *Dhanadhara/Ṛṇadhara here et seq; see E s.v. on Rāhula see Lamotte 1976:74n. and ref.; Foucher 1949:370 n. 230.

R names the chief queen as Gopā here et seq; agreeing with *Lv*. *Mv* and most sources (e.g. *Bc* 2:26) identify her as Yaśodharā, save that the earliest sources refers to her only as "Rāhula's mother" (Bareau 1974:272-73, *DPPN* s.v. Rāhulamātā). Senart speculates (1882:306-8) that the name Gopā is a late substitution, affecting an equivalency to the Kṛṣṇa myth, as is the harem as well. *Msv*, however, names her among three wives (Lamotte 1958:728; see also Durt 1982:114); *Mpps* says that Gopā was first, but she was sterile (2:1003-4). Materials collected at Bareau 1982. See also *Mpps* 5:2236 and ref. n. 2; Thomas 1949:48-50; Foucher 1949:82, 83; E s.v. the various names.

112. *Mv* cites "tradition" in relating that Rāhula was reborn from Tuṣita (1:153:14-15), and later relates the same as fact (2:159:1). At *Mv* 1:154:3 (and E s.v. *aupapāduka*), correct *āsannatathā* to *āsan-tathā*: it must be that Rāhula's birth is asserted to be apparitional, rather than denied. *Bc* 2:49 describes the birth as quite ordinary. For the time of the birth see *Mpps* 2:1001-2n., Lamotte 1958:734-36: according to some sources, the birth occurred long before the Bodhisattva's departure from home; this taints the reputation of the mother, and "apparitional rebirth" is in part an answer to it.

113. The story of Megha and Prakṛti is alluded to here; the tale is told at *Mv* 1:232:13-234:15. The maid Prakṛti declines an offer by Megha to purchase five of her seven utpala (blue lotus flowers) as an offering to Buddha Dīpaṁkara. Instead, she gives them in return for the promise of marriage, promising in turn not to hinder his *bodhicitta.* The incident is absent in the corresponding *Nk* account of Sumedha (2ff), but a corresponding tale occurs in the *Apadāna*; see Bareau 1982:50. See also n. 89 above.

114. "Distress" (*vinipāta*) is code for a lower state of rebirth. The total number of consorts is only forty thousand in Pali commentaries (*Nk* 75, Thomas 1949:48). *Mv* 2:48:7 refers to "many thousands". The total number here may well be meant to correspond to *Lv* 108:31-23: eighty-four thousand. Foucher discusses expansion of the number at 1949:88.

115. "Creates emanations (*nirmitān abhinirmiṇati*): this is well attested as a capability of a Buddha in *Mv* and *Lv*. This observation upon harem life does not appear elsewhere, but at *Lv* 196:19-20 the Bodhisattva multiplies his bodies for the village maid Sujātā. *PWP* (55) discusses the same issue of his home life; the five sense-pleasures are likened to a magician's creations. Parallels to the dalliance of Kṛṣṇa with the gopis are discussed Senart 1882:291, 304-8.

116. For "servant" *upasthāyaka,* R Tib has "son of the Śākyas" *śākyaputra*; but "servant" is the common term of reference for the Bodhisattva's groom. On the great departure see Bareau 1962:21-24, 1974:246-60; *Sbhv* 1:84-93; Thomas 1949, ch. 5; *Lv* ch. 15; *Nk* 81-87; *Mpps* 1:7-11; Foucher 1949:103-7. See also Lamotte 1958:718-19 for discussion of sources. The age of the Bodhisattva is 29 (Thomas 1949:51).

117. This childhood incident is mentioned here, as the text indicates, because it prefigures the great departure. The Bodhisattva sits under a jambu (rose-apple) tree and falls into meditation, attaining the first trance (*Lv* ch. 11: all four trances). As the day wears on, the shade of the tree does not leave him (*chāyā bodhisattvaṁ na jahāti, Mv* 2:45:14). For the documents, see Durt 1982. See also Bareau 1974:218-37, Nanamoli 1972:8, *Bc* ch., 5, *Sbhv* 75-78, Thomas 1949:44-46, Foucher 1949:92-95, E s.v. *vihahanatā* from *Bbh*, *Nk* 74-75.

118. R Tib, losing a word, reads "does not dislike his relatives". The sūtra version of the incident of the visions does not entail going to a park (Nanamoli 1972:9, cp. *Mv* 2:150-51). See also Bareau 1962:16-21, *Nk* 76-79, *Sbhv* 67-75, *Bc* ch. 3, Foucher 1949:95-97, Thomas 1949:51-52.

119. *Mv* specifies midnight, and has son Rāhula enter the womb at that time (2:159:3, 13). Other ref. n. 116 above. Cp. reasons for his departure at *Mv* 2:117, 161-62, and *Bc* 6:15-24.

120. Ref. *ibid. Mv*: Kaṇṭhaka neighs loudly, but the gods have put the city to sleep; the doors are opened by yakṣas (2:160-61). In *Nk* (83) the gate is opened by a deva. *Bc* (5:82): he is borne in flight by yakṣas; the gates have opened by themselves.

121. Ref. *ibid.* Fa agrees with *Mv* (2:165:1), R with *Lv* (163:27).

122. The "usages of the nobles" (*āryavaṁśa*), or the customs of a renunciate, are (*Ak* 6:7cd): contentment with the clothing, alms, and bedding of a renunciate and delight in the path to nirvāṇa. See also section 146 and n. following.

123. So Fa: *kinnara*, a creature half human and half horse. R: *amanuṣya*, a ghost or spirit. In *Mv* (2:165:19) and *Lv* (164:2), the hair is taken up by the Trāyatriṁśa gods.

124. R thus interpolates the interpretation current among the schools: the six years of austerities undergone by Śākyamuni (which proved to be irrelevant to the attainment of awakening) were the karmic result of his denigration of Buddha Kāśyapa with those words. So *Msv* 1:*27-28, 217-18; *Apadāna* 1:301, v. 29-30. *Msv* refers to the Madhyamāgama for the full story; cp. Majjhima no. 81, vol. 2; *Nk* 51, *Mv* 1:317-38, Sbhv 2:22-30, *Jātaka* 1:43, *Mpps* 1:22-23n. Jyotipāla says, "Where is the awakening" etc., and the potter Ghaṭikāra (or Nandipāla) drags him by the hair to see the Buddha Kāśyapa. This is the Bodhisattva's last birth before Tuṣita (see section 114 following).

For earlier discussion of the curious incident of Jyotipāla, see McDermott 1989, Mus 1933 : 813-16.

The earliest interpretation of the six years of austerities—that they demonstrate a wrong way in order to point up the Middle Way—is adduced by *Up* at sections 115-16 following. In *Msv*, *Apadāna*, and elsewhere the six years are part of the set of "karmic connections" discussed by *Up* in Part Three following.

"Speech with a hidden intention" (*saṁdhā-vacana*): see Majjhima 1:503:17, *Lotus* 349-50, Lamotte 1958:55, Conze 1967 s.v. *Saṁdhāya*, E s.v. Ruegg 1969 index s.v. *abhiprāya* etc. ("arrière-pensée"), Broido 1984. See also section 127 following.

125. In earlier versions "Jyotipāla and the potter are " childhood companions" (*Mv* 1:319:11 *vayasya, Sbhv* 2:23:2 *vayasyaka,* Majjhima 2:1:46:5 *sahāya*). "Well-to-do" (*mahāśāla*) describes the family of Jyotipāla in older versions; see the gloss at *Sbhv* 2:22:3-4.

R Tib has "Jyotimāla"; R Ch seems to have "Jyotis". The five companions are an invention by the *Up.*

126. So R; Fa apparently misconstrues: "Alas, if these sentient beings are to mature their stores of merit..."

127. Skt *prajñāpāramitā-jñāna-niśyandena upāyakauśalyena.* His original commitment (*dam bcas pa, pratijñā*) is of course of the generation of the awakening thought. Fa renders this with a term (*yi dam*) used by the *Bbh* for obligation (*samādāna*) to the Bodhisattva vow.

Skill in means is also described as "the outcome [*niśyanda,* translated "outpouring"] of the perfection of wisdom" as *PWA* 109; R has been harmonized with that passage. See also the explanation *ibid.* 111-12, based on *PWRg* 3:7. See also *PWA* 273, based upon *PWRg* 28:6, a verse with some difficulties that seems to say that all sources of means (*upāya-mūla*) and ways to gnosis (*jñāna-naya-dvāra*) are issued (*prasūta*) from the perfection of wisdom.

128. In the *Mv*, Jyotipāla and Ghaṭikāra are found on the edge of a lotus pond (1:320:17-18), Jyotipāla putting his long hair into a brahman's chignon after an ablution, when Ghaṭikāra seizes him by the chignon to go to see and show honor to (*darśanāyopasaṁkramantaṁ paryupāsanāya*) the Buddha.

129. "Having no impact" comes from the *Mv* account, in which Jyotipāla resists (1:321:11).

130. Skt *Avaivartikacakra-dhāraṇī-vajrapada-sarvadharmānutpāda-bodhisattvapitaka-dharmaparyāya*. Mv mentions instruction "with a doctrinal discourse" (*dhārmayā kathayā*, 1:322:6-7), following bestowal upon Jyotipāla of refuge and lay precepts. Jyotipāla later becomes a monk; still later, he resolves to become a Buddha and receives confirmation that he will do so (1:330, 331-32).

131. "Bound to one more birth only" (*ekajāti-pratibaddha*): a phrase used by *Lv* (8:19) to describe the Bodhisattva in Tuṣita; here it refers to the life before Tuṣita (which is the last birth proper, see section 76 above). So also *Mpps* 1:267. The Bodhisattva endowed with perfection of wisdom and skill in means is defined as a once returner at *PWP* 69; see also on Bodhisattva stages.

The Bodhisattva should not "grow obsessed with excessive regret" for a misdeed, because he can rectify the fault if *bodhicitta* is still intact (*Upāli* 39).

132. "To confute them": the argument derives from *Mv* 2:127:17-128:1. The daily food that is itemized corresponds to *Mv, Lv* and *Bc* (12:96); *Nk* lacks the jujube; *Mpps* corresponds to *Nk*; Majjhima (Nanamoli 1972:18) is corrupt, detailing what he ate later, when breaking his fast. References *Mpps* 1:12n.

133. R Tib gives the number four million, two hundred-thousand. The terminology ". . . devoted to wretched (practices, *lūhādhimuktā devatā*)" derives from *Mv* 2:131:5; see also *Lv* 193:13.

134. "The path cannot be gained with the body emaciated, impotent (*kṛśeṇa, durbalena*; Mv 2:131:5; cp *Lv* 193:9). The Bodhisattva takes food from the cow-girl Sujātā (but she is not mentioned by name in the early versions). In the *Mv*, intervention by devas is needed (but *Mv* translation at 2:126, which indicates that he approves of fasting, is incorrect; rather, he has promised *pratijānāmi* to fast, *Mv* 2:131:3, followed by *Lv* 193:16-19); the gods and the local people expect him to fast. See also Bareau 1963:1:55-61, Nanamoli 1972:18, *Nk* 90-94, Thomas 1949:70-71, Foucher 1949:139-41 and references.

"Nirvāṇize": see Skt, reference n. 139 below.

135. On the seven or thirty-seven aids to awakening (*bodhi-pakṣa*), beginning with the four applications of mindfulness, see *PWP* 671. Other texts offer other explanations: Sujātā intended the offerings for a tree deity in hope of bearing a son (*Nk* 91); she has been the Bodhisattva's mother in five hundred past lives (*Mv* 2:206:17). The explanation by *Up* resembles that of *Bc* 12:112: she (called Nandabālā) becomes capable of awakening (*bodhiprāptau samartho 'bhūt*). *Lv* also confirms her future Buddhahood (195:9-12). In early versions, she and her family take refuge (Bareau 1963:1:127-34).

136. *Viraja*: "dustless", free from passion. Fa reads "Vairocana", doubtless an error. No other source predicts Buddhahood for Svastika. See *Mv* 2:131:12, 264:6; *Lv* 207:27; *Nk* 95; *Bc* 12:119; Thomas 1949:71; Foucher 1949:147. On the role of kuśa grass in vedic rites see Bareau 1963:1:61.

137. R would appear to have demoted Māra from ruler of many world-systems to

ruler of one. In terms of Mount Sumeru cosmology, R is correct: Māra's heaven floats above the peak of a Sumeru system and its four continents (Tatz 1977:103). The following two sections support Fa, however, and in *Mv* (2:314:4-15, 321) Māra who is ruler of a *trisāhasra* offers the Bodhisattva dominion over four continents.

Māra does not appear in vinaya accounts of the awakening, save in the late *Sbhv* (1:113-19). On the battle with him see *Suttanipāta* 425-49, Nanamoli 1972:19-21, Thomas 1949: 71-79, *Nk* 96-101, *Mv* 2:404:20-419:15, *Lv* ch. 20-22, *Bc* ch. 13, Foucher 1949:151-60, Senart 1882:162-207, Lamotte 1958:731, *Mpps* 1:12 and n. 2, *ibid.* 2:880-84. On the figure of Māra see also Wayman 1959.

138. "Intermediate cause": *antara-hetu*? Cp. the phrase *bodhi-hetu*, corresponding to Fa *nirvāṇa-hetu*, at *Lv* 119:12 and discussion; *Mv* 1:536, n. to line 6; E s.v. *hetu* (2) on the adverbial use of *hetu*.

Many among Māra's host have stores of merit; see *Mv* 2:315:10. See also *Lv* 218:8-9: seeing his lion's play, the hosts of Māra generate *bodhicitta*, etc. *PWP* 40, 148: "lion's play" is a brilliant, earth-shaking *samādhi* (commented upon at *Mpps* 1:431-52). On "lion" see also *Mv* 2:281, 309-14, 316:20; on "play" see *Mv* 1:178:8, *Lv* 130:19 (the "play of his great skill in means"), E s.v. *vikrīḍita*.

139. The world is likewise illumined at parallel passages of *Mv* (2:313ff) and *Lv* (218:10ff), and *Lv* also credits the light with speech. "Will nirvāṇize" (*nirvāpayiṣyati*): cp. *Lv* 218:22.

140. *Mv* verse (2:342:20): "thirty square yojanas (of flowers thrown by the gods); *Mv* prose (2: 315:4ff): an army of "many yojanas". Cp. *Lv* 222:29: *samantāntā dasītir yojana* (correct E *Grammar* 19:38).

Mahorāga: land-serpents. *Kumbhāṇḍa*: a class of demons.

141. *Up* may be using the plural in this last paragraph in order to show the parallelism of the careers of all Buddhas. At this point in the *Mv* account of Dīpaṁkara (1:230:12-231:2), he remains in the lotus position in which he attained awakening, receiving homage from the same divinities and acceding to their request to teach doctrine; the terms "elated", etc. may come from there. Description of the sitting position, etc. follows *Mv* 2:15-16. See also *Mv* 3:281:4-7; *Nk* 105-6; *Bc* 14:94; *Lv* 274:20, 279:25-26. See also "seven days" discussed Bareau 1963:1:98-100.

The gods described as *rūpāvacāra-praśāntacarya* reside well above Māra's realm of desire. They represent states of trance; see Tatz 1977:107, 111, 172.

142. On the misconception that Brahmā is "the creator" see Tatz 1977:34-35. The Bodhisattva agrees to the request by Brahmā, according to *Mv* (3:318:14-15), because of his compassion, the request itself, and his resolve made seven eons before; *Lv* (292:30-293:2): because of the request itself and his compassion. But cp. *Mv* 3:447:1-8, misplaced verses that may indicate teaching unrequested. See also Kloppenborg 1973:6-7, Nanamoli 1972:37-39, *Nk* 111, Thomas 1949:81-86, *Bc* 14:95-103, *Sbhv* 1:129-30, Bareau 1963:1:135-43, *Mpps* 1:13 and 55-63, Foucher 1949:189-91.

143. R Tib reads "sixty-eight thousand".

144. "Karmic connections" (* *karma-saṁtati*) is literally "continuations of *karma*". Cp. the nine "results of misdeeds" (*āpatti-vipāka*) at *Mpps* 1:5-07-17, and refs. *ibid.* to lists from *Msv*, *Apadāna*, etc., including a passage of *Daśadharmaka* sūtra of the Ratnakūṭa (511n.), further discussion at Lamotte 1976:294-98. A similar list is known to the *Laṅka* (207). Cp. also *Mpps* 3:1661-90 for a set of apparent misdeeds committed by the Buddha in his last existence.

145. For the Sanskrit see *Lv* 312:18. Kumārajīva makes nearly the same argument at *Mpps* 1:513-14. On the question of the Buddha's suffering see also *Ak* 4:212 n. 2; *Hob* 234a.

146. R: "he displays *karma*". This passage of R is translated at *Hob* 235, the translation reproduced at *Mpps* 1:511n. ("King of healing", however, is mistranslated and lost in R Ch; on it see section 57 and n. 76 above.)

147. According to the analysis of this tale by the *Bbh* (at Tatz 1986:214-15), these elements must be present for an act of murder to be ethical: someone about to commit a deed of immediate retribution, no other means to prevent it, the Bodhisattva aware of the consequences for himself, his own attitude not unwholesome but compassionate, and mastery of skill in means.

In the version of the *Mv* (etc., references and *Mv* Skt at *Mpps* 1:283-4n.; cp. also *Jātaka* no. 463, vol. 4), the Bodhisattva as *sārthavāha* Mahākāruṇika sacrifices his own life to save his companions from shipwreck, when the sacrifice is demanded by a deity of the sea.

"Jambu Continent" here refers to the mainland of India.

The tale is intended to adduce the deed in a past life that resulted in Śākyamuni being pierced by a thorn; see following. In the *Apadāna* the thorn is explained by a past life in which the Bodhisattva was a king who slew a man with a spear (1:300, v. 21-22; see also *Mpps* 1:508n.) The Jain work *ṣaḍdarśana-samuccaya* (cited *ibid.*) quotes the Buddha as saying: "Ninety-one eons ago I slew a man with a spear/ The ripened *karma* of which is this stab in the foot, O monks."

148. We may understand from this that according to *Up* an auspicious eon (*bhadra-kalpa*) contains five hundred Buddhas. In length, a *bhadrakalpa* is a *mahākalpa*; see n. 42 above. According to Pali tradition, five Buddhas appear in it (Childers 1875 s.v. *kappa*); so also *Gaṇḍavyūha* (E s.v. *bhadrakalpa*). *Mv*: five is emended to one thousand (3:330:5 and n.) *Lv* 299:3: one thousand/var. one hundred. *Vk* (Lamotte 1976:266 and n.): one thousand. *PWA* 181: twenty thousand. *PWP* 68-69: no number specified. On past Buddhas see ref. n. 51 above.

Although the Bodhisattva is prepared to go to hell for his deed, and in fact says that he did so when relating this deed to his disciples in the *Apadāna* (1:300, v. 21b), it does not appear that he actually does so according to *Up*. "Saṁsāra was curtailed (*parāṅmukha*)"; cp. section 35 and n. 48, 49 above. *PWP* 168-69 notes that the Bodhisattva, because of his great compassion, is willing to roast in hell for another sentient being. Commenting upon this, *Mpps* (cited *ibid.* n.) addresses the question of whether the Bodhisattva can take upon himself the maturation of someone else's *karma*. In *Up* he can, of course, since he himself performs the deed. But it does not seem that he actually goes to hell, because the motivation for the deed is not unwholesome. *Bbh* (cited n. 147) describes the deed as generating much merit. *Up* probably means us to understand that he dwells in a brahma world as a result.

149. Maudgalyāyana is referred to as "master" (*āyuṣman*) rather than "elder" (*sthavīra*) by Fa at the last occurrence only; see n. 30 above. He is famed for magical power; see ref. n. 50 above.

The incident occurs while the Buddha is walking in a wood (*Mpps* 1:510; other ref. *ibid.* 508n.) The Jain work cited n. 147 above implies that he was restlessly peripatetic. The forty converts are added to the account by *Up*.

150. The account of this incident appears to come from the *Msv* (2:47:7-14): for

an illness, *guḍaharītakīm*, that may be gastroenteritis, Jīvaka compounds a purgative from thirty-two *utpala*, the blue lotus, which the Buddha snuffs (*ghrāta*). R's Skt *utpalahastagandha*, a medicine "smelling like a handful of *utpala*"(?) is otherwise unattested. Textual corruptions of the medicine in *Sbhv* (2:90-93) and *Mahīśāsaka-vinaya* (cited *Hob* 233a-b) result in "thirty-two ounces of ghee" or "infusion" (*ghṛta, nārācaghṛta*).

Jīvaka is physician to the court of Rājagṛha and the Buddhist community; see *DPPN*, E s.v. He is entitled "king of physicians" (*vaidya-rāja*) at *Msv* 2:42:4 and other places.

The illness is described as recompense for a past deed at *Sbhv* ibid.; *Apadāna* 1:301, v. 28; and *Msv* 1:*27, 218. *Apadāna*: "I was a physician who purged a merchant's son,/ For which deed I now have diarrhea". Not receiving his fee from the merchant for previous consultations, the Bodhisattva damaged the son's intestines with too strong a medicine.

As a karmic connection, this illness is not part of the *Mpps* list of nine (1:506-11).

The earliest sources contain only vague references to illness of the Buddha. Near the time of the parinirvāṇa, he falls ill and suppresses the illness by himself (Bareau 1963:2:1:6:3); Nanamoli 1972:302, from Dīgha). Aṅguttara refers to a recovery earlier in his life (*ibid.* 195-96).

151. Fa "cannot be pacified" (*asamitavya*), R Tib "cannot remain alive" (*ajīvitavya*).

In the ceremonies of monastic ordination (though not in the text of the *Prātimokṣa*), the medicine prescribed for general use by monastics is *pūtimukta*, "excrements". See section 147 following; also the article by J. May at *Hob* 329a-335a, Banerjee 1957:128-32.

152. Evidently, the avoidance of other medicine is regarded by *Up* as one of the *āryavaṁśa*, perhaps a version of the problematic fourth (see n. 122 above). More usually, it is fourth in another list, that of the four reliances (*niśraya*) of religious life (the first three: sleeping at the foot of a tree, begging one's food, and wearing rags).

The dilemma indicated here is that waiving a rule for monks in this instance would precipitate a general decline in adherence to it in future.

153. "Pure Abodes" (*śuddhāvāsa*): several levels of deity of the realm of form corresponding to the highest stage of trance; ref. n. 141 above.

154. The Buddha's failure to get alms in a brahman village is related in the *Piṇḍasūtra*; discussion, references *Mpps* 1:457-58. As a karmic connection it is part of the *Msv* and other lists (*ibid.* 509n., 511), but not that of the *Apadāna*.

155. R Tib omits. "Possession" or "inspiration" (*anvāviśati*) by Māra is part of all earlier accounts (*Mpps* 1:458n.)

156. According to the older accounts they "remain joyous, like the *ābhāsvara* gods" (*Mpps* 1:458-59n.). The point of the tale is to teach (1) equanimity in the face of adversity, and (2) the healthiness of eating only once daily (*Hob* 160a).

157. "Well-to-do": *mahāśālin*; this may be the proper name of the village. In older Sanskrit sources it is called Śālā; in Pali sources it is called Pañcasālā, "five *sāla* trees" (*Mpps* 1:458n.)

158. Cañcā-māṇavikā is hired by brahmans to pretend to pass nights at the Jeta Grove for some months and then to confront Śākyamuni during a lecture with a pregnancy, feigned with the aid of a wooden bowl. *Up* seems to follow versions (e.g. *Msv* 1:161-63) in which the god Indra causes the bowl to fall to earth; the girl is

banished and goes to hell when she dies. In other versions she falls to hell immediately, or burns alive. Ref. *Mpps* 1:123n.; see also Thomas 1949:111, Foucher 1949:278-79, *DPPN* s.v. Ciñcā.

This incident is by some accounts a karmic recompense for having slandered religious figures in past lives. See *Apadāna* 1:299, v. 7-9; *Msv* 1:*24, *29, 212:9-216:2, *Mpps* 1:508. The Bodhisattva went to hell for the deeds; this incident is a residue of the *karma*.

159. R Tib omits. Sundarī/Sundarikā is a non-buddhist *parivrājikā* who is directed by her conferers to pretend to pass a night with the Buddha. Thereafter, they hire thugs to slay her and conceal the body in a rubbish pit nearby. For one week, until the assassins are discovered, the Buddhists are blamed for her death. Ref. *Mpps* 1:507-8, *DPPN* Sundarī (3), *Jātaka* introduction to no. 285 (vol. 2), Nanamoli 1972:140-41, Thomas 1949:111-12, Foucher 1949:279-80, *Sbhv* 1:207-9.

This incident as the residue of a past deed: see *Msv* 1:*22-24, *Apādana* 1:299-300 (v. 3-6), *Mpps* 1:509-10n.

160. The four assemblies (*catuṣpariṣad*) are male and female monastics, and male and female householders.

161. Fa: "brahmans and householders"; but one person, in *Msv* named Agnidatta, is responsible in the older accounts. The place is Vairambha (*ibid.*), according to Rhys-Davids "in Kośala" (cited Mochizuki 1940:36-37). During the twelfth rainy season of the Buddha's ministry, a brahman invites the community but neglects to feed them; the countryside is in famine and the Buddha declines to beg. In some versions the patron is said to be under the influence of Māra. Ref. *Mpps* 1:124-25; see also *Msv* 1:24-48, Thomas 1949:118. See the comparison of Pali and Dharmaguptaka versions and translation of the latter by Pradhan 1945:2-4, 18-20.

For the incident as recompense for a past deed see *Apadāna* 1:300-1, v. 25-26; *Msv* 1:*26-27, 216-17; *Mpps* 1:509-10n.

162. R Tib: "eats food during the three-month rains".

163. "Most excellent taste" is mark number 26 of 32 in the list of *PWP* (585): "He has (taste) conductors which give him the most excellent taste. . ." More detail is provided by *Mpps* (1:278), e.g. "the two extremities of his throat secrete an ambrosia that concentrates all savors." Ref. to *Mv*, *Lv*, etc. E s.v. *lakṣaṇa*. See also *Aa* 48-102 on the marks.

164. *Up* is evidently aware of versions in which the gods enhance the nutritive value of the horse-feed (*Milinda*, etc., ref. *Mpps* 1:125 n. 1). On seven days' digestion of *amṛta* see Lamotte 1976:312-13.

165. R Tib adds: "among the Thus Come Ones". This may be conflation, but cp. the *Jātaka* account (no. 430, vol. 3): "Oh the contented character of Tathāgatas!"

166. The patron who fails to deliver is not blamed in any account of this incident, but cp. the *Dhammapada* commentary (Burlingame 1921:193-94): five hundred non-monastic beggars evince disgusting greed while eating. Cp. also *Msv* 1:43.

167. "Observing Uposatha day" (*upavāsa-stha*): days of the lunar cycle on which monastics recite *prātimokṣa* while householders observe semi-monastic precepts and audit discourses; see *CPD* s.v. *uposatha*, Mpps. 2:825-26n.

This incident comes from the *Śaikṣa-sūtra* (also Majjhima 1:353-59), in which the Buddha commands Ānanda to teach the seven limbs of awakening (ref. *Mpps* 1:244, 2:942-44, 3:1649). The Buddha's back is troubled by (the humor) wind, and the brahman Devahita cures it with a cold-water massage; ref. *ibid.* 1:509n. As a karmic connected see *ibid.*; also Chavannes 1910:1:423-24; *Apadāna* 1:301, v. 27.

The seven limbs of awakening (*bodhyaṅga*) are mindfulness, investigation into dharmas, vigor, joyous zest, tranquillity, concentration, and evenmindedness (*PWP* 668).

168. The four elements (*bhūta*) are earth, air, fire and water. For this phrase (*audārikabhūtakāya-pariniṣpanna*), see ref. E s.v. *audārika*, esp. *Mv* 2:277:18: Māra says, "The śramaṇa Gautama has a gross body born from his parents; mine is a mind-made body".

169. The dynasty (*rāja-vaṁśa*) ends when Siddhārtha, an only son, renounces home life. Later, the Śākyas are massacred by Virūḍaka; see the study by Bareau (1981). On the reaction of the Buddha see *Mpps* 1:511 and ref. *ibid.* 508-9n.; also Thomas 1949:139-40 (how the Buddha tried to save them, according to Pali sources), Foucher 1949:237.

170. Divinities (*devaputra*) are unlikely to be murderous, since they have attained the station by purified morality, but they may be misguided and believe in the annihilation of consciousness upon death (*ucchedavāda*), thereby denying the working of *karma*.

"As a residue" (*avaśeṣeṇa*): so Fa, as accords with *Msv*, etc.; see n. 158 above. R: "as a result of" (*vaśena*). According to the *Apadāna* (1:300, v. 23-24) and *Msv* (1:*25-26), the Buddha admits to having killed fish when he was a fisherman's son. See also *Mpps* 1:509-10n.

171. R Tib: "one hundred forms of abuse". This incident is not part of the other lists of karmic connection. See *DPPN* s.v. Bharadvāja (4) and references; esp. *Suttanipāta*, sutta no. 7 (pp. 30-35): A brahman of the Aggika-bharadvāja clan hails the Buddha insultingly as shave-pate, śramaṇa, and outcaste, but he is ordained at the end of the Buddha's response.

172. Fa adds, "and they hold to ethics", but this belongs to the following section.

The past-life tales alluded to are legion; see *Jātaka* indices s.v. Devadatta; e.g. Devadatta as the brahman Jūjaka in the Vessantara-jātaka (no. 547, vol. 6).

173. Three incidents: (1) The assassins are sixteen archers of King Ajātaśatru. *Sbhv* consolidates this with the incident of the catapult. (2) The elephant Dhanapāla/Nālāgiri is maddened and set upon the Buddha by Devadatta. (3) Fa alludes to the version in which hired assassins use a catapult, R to the more common version in which Devadatta himself looses a boulder from a hillside. The rock breaks apart before reaching him, but a fragment injures the foot of the Buddha and this is his "residue of *karma*". Ref. *Mpps* 2:874. See also *Sbhv* 2:166-70 (the boulder); *Bc* 21:40-58, *Sbhv* 2:189-91, Chavannes 1911:3:101 (the elephant).

In the lists of karmic connections in *Mpps* (1:510) and *Msv* (1:*25), only the boulder incident is given; *Apadāna* has all three (1:300, v. 15-20); other lists *Mpps* 1:510n.

174. Fa's "ambitious" (*yaśas-kāma*) is preferable to R's "benevolent" (*hita-kāma*); cp. *Mpps* 3:1545. Devadatta's ambition is to inherit leadership of the Buddhist community; for his schismatic efforts to that end see *Sbhv* entire, *Mpps* 2:868-78; on the Buddha's refusal see *ibid* 3:1671-74, *DPPN* 1008. Devadatta is associated with Ajātaśatru, who kills his father to accede to kingship.

175. "Attain illumination" (*āloka-lābha*) is a stage that follows attainment of belief

or adherence (*adhimukti*), according to later formulations of the Bodhisattva path; those are the first two stages of the beginner's stage of adherence (*adhimukticaryābhūmi*; Mhv 896-901). *Msa* 14:24 and commentary may bear on this also: "illumination" is glossed as "the conviction that comes of considering the *dharmas* of the Buddha"; cp. also a parallel passage of Majjhima noted Lévi, *Msa* tr. 166.

176. The ending by Fa bears out the older interpretation of M. Müller: the Lord is enraptured. Such is the Skt of *PWA* etc.; Chinese and Tibetan translators construe "enraptured" (*āttamanāḥ*) with the audience only, or the audience and the Lord. See Kajiyama 1977.

177. On the enactment of a new language standard for translation (incorporated in *Mhv* and *Sgra-sbyor*) by these and other scholars, see *Sgra-sbyor* introduction and Bu-ston tr. 2:196-97.

BIBLIOGRAPHY AND ABBREVIATIONS

Aa=*Abhisamayālaṁkāra*. Translation, Sanskrit-Tibetan indexes by Edward Conze. Serie Orientale Roma 6 (1954).

Ak=*Abhidharmakośa*. Translated by Louis de La Vallée Poussin, *L'Abhidharmakośa de Vasubandhu*. Paris: Geuthner, 1923-26. 6 volumes and index.

Anesaki, Masaku. 1918. Docetism (Buddhist). In *Encyclopaedia of Religion and Ethics*, edited by James Hastings, 4:835-40. New York: Scribner's.

Apadāna=*Therāpadāna*. Edited by Mary E. Lilley. PTS 1925.

Asaṅga, *Bodhisattvabhūmi*. See s.v.

Aśokāvadāna. Translated by Jean Przyluski in *La légende de l'Emperor Aśoka dans les textes indiens et chinois*. AMG 31. Paris, 1923.

Aṣṭa=*Aṣṭasāhasrikā Prajñāpāramitā*. Translated by Edward Conze as *The Perfection of Wisdom in Eight Thousand Lines and its Verse Summary*. Bolinas, California: Four Seasons Foundation, 1973.

Aśvaghoṣa. *Buddhacarita*. Chapters 1-14 edited and translated by E.H. Johnston, Lahore, 1936. Chapters 15-28 *idem* in *Acta Orientalia* 15 (1937).

——*Saundarananda*. Edited and translated by E.H. Johnston, Lahore, 1928. Reprinted Delhi: Motilal Banarsidass, 1975.

Banerjee, Ankul Chandra. 1957. *Sarvāstivāda Literature*. Calcutta: by the author.

Bareau, André. 1962. La Jeunesse du Buddha. In *BEFEO* 61.

——1963 et seq. *Recherches sur La Biographie du Buddha dans les Sūtrapiṭaka et les Vinayapiṭaka Anciens*. 2 vol. Paris: École française d'Extrême-Orient.

——1969. The Superhuman Personality of Buddha and its Symbolism in the *Mahāparinirvāṇasūtra* of the Dharmaguptaka. In *Myths and Symbols*, edited by Joseph M. Kitagawa and Charles H. Long, 9-21. Chicago: University of Chicago Press.

——1981. Le Massacre des Śākya: Essai d'Interprétation. In *BEFEO* 69:45-73.

——1982. Un Personnage. In *Indological and Buddhist Studies*, ed. L.A. Hercus, et al, 31-59. Canberra: Faculty of Asian Studies.

Basham, Arthur L. 1981. The Evolution of the Concept of the Bodhisattva. In Kawamura 1981:19-59.

Bbh = *Bodhisattvabhūmi*.

Bc = Aśvaghoṣa. *Buddhacarita*.

BEFEO = *Bulletin de l'École française d'Extrême-Orient.*
Bendall, Cecil. 1922. See Śāntideva, *Śikṣāsamuccaya.*
Bhadramāyākāravyākaraṇa. Edited and translated by Konstanty Régamey. Warsaw Society of Science and Letters: Publications of the Oriental Commission no. 3, 1938.
Birnbaum, Raoul. 1979. *The Healing Buddha.* Boulder: Shambhala.
Bodhisattvabhūmi. Edited by Nalinaksha Dutt. Patna: Jayaswal Institute, 1966. Chapter on Ethics translated by Tatz 1986.
Broido, Michael M. 1984. Abhiprāya and Implication in Tibetan Linguistics. In *Journal of Indian Philosophy* 12:1:1-33.
BTI=*Buddhist Text Information.*
Burrow, T. 1933-35. Iranian Words in the Karoṣṭhi Documents from Chinese Turkestan. In *Bulletin of the School of Oriental and African Studies* 7.
Buddhaghoṣa. *Visuddhimagga.* Edited by Henry Clarke Warren, revised by Dharmananda Kosambi. Cambridge: Harvard University Press, 1950. Translated by Nanamoli as *The Path of Purification.* Kandy: Buddhist Publication Society, 1975.
Burlingame, E.W. 1921. *Buddhist Legends* (the *Dhammapada* commentary). Cambridge: Harvard University Press.
Bu-ston Rin-cheng-grub. *History of Buddhism.* Edited by Lokesh Chandra in *The Collected Works of Bu-ston,* vol. 24. New Delhi 1971. Translated by E. Obermiller. Heidelberg 1931. Reprinted 2 vol. in 1. Tokyo: Suzuki Research Foundation, n.d.
Caillat, Colette. 1984. Prohibited Speech and *Subhāsita* in the Theravāda Tradition. In *Indologica Taurinensia* 12.
Candrakīrti. See *Pp.*
Chang, Garma et al. 1983. *A Treasury of Mahāyāna Sūtras.* University Park: Pennsylvania State University Press.
Chavannes, Édouard. 1910-34. *Cinq Cents Conte et Apologues Extraits du Tripiṭaka Chinois.* 4 vol. Paris: Leroux.
Childers, R.C. 1975. *A Dictionary of the Pali Language.* London: Trübner.
Conze, Edward. 1960. *The Prajñāpāramitā Literature.* Reprinted 's-Gravenhage: Mouton.
——1962. *Buddhist Thought in India.* London: Allen & Unwin.
——1964. *Buddhist Texts Through the Ages.* Oxford: Cassirer.
——1967. *Materials for a Dictionary of the Prajñāpāramitā Literature.* Tokyo: Susuki Research Foundation.
——1968. The Composition of the Aṣṭasāhasrikā Prajñāpāramitā. In 1968b:168-84.

——1968a. The Development of Prajñāpāramitā Thought. In 1968b.
——1968b, *Thirty Years of Buddhist Studies: Selected Essays.* Columbia: University of South Carolina Press.
——See also *Aa*; *PW* all entries.
CPD = *A Critical Pāli Dictionary.* Edited by Dines Anderson et al. Copenhagen 1924 et seq.
Dayal, Har. 1932. *The Bodhisattva Doctrine in Buddhist Sanskrit Literature.* London: Trübner.
Dbh = *Daśabhūmika-sūtra.* Edited by Johannes Rahder in *Le Muséon* 39 (1926). Translated by Megamu Honda. In Śaṭapiṭaka Series 74.
DPPN = *Dictionary of Pāli Proper Names.* G.P. Malalasekera. 2 vol. London: PTS, 1960.
Durt, Hubert. 1982. La "Visite aux Laboureurs" et La "Méditation sous L'Arbre *Jambu*". In *Indological and Buddhist Studies,* ed. L.A. Hercus, et al. 95-120. Canberra: Faculty of Asian Studies.
E = Edgerton, *Dictionary.*
EB = *Encyclopaedia of Buddhism.* Edited by G.P. Malalasekera, et al. Government of Ceylon, 1961 et seq.
Edgerton, Franklin. 1953. *Buddhist Hybrid Grammar and Dictionary.* 2 vol. New Haven: Yale University Press.
Ensink, J., edited and translated. 1952. *The Question of Rāṣṭrapāla.* J.J. Tijl.
Fa = Fa-ch'eng version of *Up.* See above Introduction, section 1.
Finot, Louis. 1932. Mahāparinibbānasutta et Cullavagga. In *Indian Historical Quarterly* 8:241-46.
Foucher, A. 1949. *La Vie du Bouddha.* Paris: Payot.
Frauwallner, E. 1956. *The Earliest Vinaya and the Beginnings of Buddhist Literature.* Serie Orientale Roma 8.
Galloway, Brian. 1988. Sudden Enlightenment in the Abhisamayālaṁkāra, the Lalitavistara, and the Śikṣāsamuccaya. In *Wiener Zeitschrift fur die Kunde Südasiens* 32.
Granoff, Phyllis. 1986. The Miracle of Hagiography Without Miracles. In *Journal of Indian Philosophy* 14.
Hara, Minoru. 1980. A Note on the Buddha's Birth Story. In *Indianisme et Bouddhism,* 143-57. Louvain-la-Neuve: Institut Orientaliste.
Harrison, Paul. 1982. Sanskrit Fragments of a Lokottaravādin Tradition. In *Indological and Buddhist Studies,* edited by L.A. Hercus, et al. 211-34. Canberra: Faculty of Asian Studies.
Harrison, Paul. 1992. Is the *Dharma-kāya* the Real "Phantom Body" of the Buddha? In Journal of the International Association of Buddhist Studies 15:1.

Hikata, Ryusho. 1958. *Suvikrāntavikrāmi-paripṛcchā Prajñāpāramitā-Sūtra.* Kyushu University, Fukuoka, Japan.

Hob = *Hōbōgirin.* Edited by Sylvain Lévi et al. Tokyo: Maison Franco-Japonaise, 1931 et seq.

Hurvitz, Leon. 1975. One Vehicle or Three? Tr. from the Japanese of Fujita Kotatsu. In *Journal of Indian Philosophy* 3:79-166.

——1976. See *Lotus.*

——See also Tsukamoto 1985.

Inaba, Shoju. 1977. On Chos-grub's Translation of the *Chieh-shên-mi-ching-shu.* In Leslie Kawamura and Keith Scott, edited, *Buddhist Thought in Asian Civilization* 105-13.

Jātaka. 6 vol. Edited by V. Fausboll. London 1877-96. Translated by E.B. Cowell et al. Cambridge 1895-1907.

K = *The Korean Buddhist Canon: A Descriptive Catalogue.* By Lewis Lancaster. Berkeley: University of California Press, 1979.

Kajiyama, Yuichi.1977. "Thus Spoke the Blessed One..." In Lancaster 1977:93-99.

Kāma-sūtra. See Vatsyayana.

Kāśyapa-parivarta. Edited by A. von Staël-Holstein. Shanghai: Commercial Press, 1926.

Kawamura. Leslie S., edited. 1981 *The Bodhisattva Doctrine in Buddhism.* Wilfrid Laurier University Press.

Kloppenborg, Ria. 1973. *The Sūtra of the Foundation of the Buddhist Order* (*Catuṣpariṣatsūtra*). Leiden: Brill.

Kp = *Kāśyapa-parivarta.*

Lalitavistara-sūtra. Edited by P.L. Vaidya. Darbhanga: Mithila Institute, 1958. See also S. Lefmann, ed. 2 vol. Halle: Verlag der Buchhandlung des Waisenhauses, 1902.

Lalou, Marcelle. 1927. La version Tibétaine du Ratnakūṭa. In *Journal Asiatique* 211.

——1953 (Ldan-dkar). Les textes bouddhiques au temps du Roi Khri-sron-lde-bcan. In *Journal Asiatique* 241.

——See also Pelliot.

Lamotte, Étienne. 1947-48. La légende du Buddha. In *Revue de L'Histoire des Religions* 134:37-71.

——1958. *Histoire du Bouddhisme Indien.* Louvain: Institut Orientaliste.

——1965. See *Śūraṁgamasamādhi-sūtra.*

——1976. See *Vimalakīrtinirdeśa-sūtra.*

——1981. Lotus et Buddha Supramundain. In *BEFEO,* pp, 31-44.

——See also *Mpps.* Przyluski 1932.

Lancaster, Lewis. 1974. The Story of a Buddhist Hero. In *Tsing Hua Journal of Chinese Studies* (*Ch'ing Hua ta hsüeh*) 10:83-89.

——1977. Edited, *Prajñāpāramitā and Related Systems.* Berkeley: University of California Press.

——1981. The Bodhisattva Concept: A Study of the Chinese Buddhist Canon. In Kawamura 1981.

——See also K.

Laṅkāvatāra-sūtra. Translated by Daisetz Teitaro Suzuki. London: Routledge, 1932.

Ldan-dkar catalogue. See Lalou 1953.

Lethcoe, Nancy R. 1977. The Bodhisattva Ideal in the *Aṣṭa* and *Pañca.* Prajñāpāramitā Sūtras. In Lancaster 1977:263-80.

Lotus sūtra = *Saddharmapuṇḍarīka-sūtra.* Translated by Leon Hurvitz as *Scripture of the Lotus Blossom of the Fine Dharma.* New York: Columbia University Press, 1976.

Lv = *Lalitavistara-sūtra.*

Mahāvastu. 3 vol. Edited by E. Senart. Paris 1882-97. Translated by J.J. Jones. PTS 1949-56.

Majjhima-nikāya. 3 vol. Edited by V. Trenckner and R. Chalmers. PTS 1888-99.

McDermott, James P. 1989. The *Kathāvatthu Niyama* Debates. In *Journal of the International Association of Buddhist Studies* 12:1.

Mhv = *Mahāvyutpatti.* 2 vol. Edited by Sakaki Ryōzaburō-. Reprinted Tokyo: Suzuki Research Foundation, 1962.

Mmk = Mañjusrīmūlakalpa. 3 vol. Edited by Gaṇapati Śāstri. Trivandrum 1920-25.

Mochizuki, Shinkō. The Places of Varṣāvasāna. In *Studies on Buddhism in Japan* 2:29-44.

Mpps = *Mahāprajñāpāramitā-śāstra.* Translated by Étienne Lamotte as *Le Traité de la Grande Vertu de Saggesse.* Louvain: Institut Orientaliste, 1949 et seq.

Msa = *Mahāyānasūtrālaṁkāra.* Edited and translated by Sylvain Lévi. Paris: Honoré Champion, 1907, 1911. Indexes compiled by Gadjin Nagao. Tokyo: Nippon Gakujutsu Shinkōkai, 1958, 1961.

Msv = *Mūlasarvāstivāda-vinaya.* Edited by Nalinaksha Dutt. In *Gilgit Manuscripts* 3:1-2, 1942 et seq. See also *Sbhv.*

Mus, Paul. 1932, 1933. Barubuḍur. In *BEFEO.*

Mv = *Mahāvastu.*

MW = M. Monier-Williams. 1899. *Sanskrit-English Dictionary.* Oxford, Clarendon Press.

Nakamura, Hajime. 1976. A Survey of Mahāyāna Buddhism with Bibliographical Notes. Part One. In *Journal of Intercultural Studies* 3:60-139.

Nanamoli. 1972. *The Life of the Buddha.* Kandy: Buddhist Publication Society.

——See also Buddhaghoṣa.

Nanjio, Bunyu. 1983. *A Catalogue of the Chinese Translation of the Buddhist Tripiṭaka.* Oxford: Oxford University Press.

Nk = *Nidānakathā.* Translated by T.W. Rhys Davids as *Buddhist Birth-Stories.* London. Trübner, 1880. Revised translation by C.A.F. Rhys Davids. London: Routledge, 1925. Cited according to 1880 translation.

O = Otani reprint of the Peking edition of the Tibetan Sacred Canon. Edited by D.T. Suzuki et al as *The Tibetan Tripiṭaka.* Tokyo-Kyoto, 1957.

O'Flaherty, Wendy Doniger. 1973. *Asceticism and Eroticism in the Mythology of Śiva.* London: Oxford.

Ogubenine, Boris. 1982. La Dakṣiṇa dans Le Ṛgveda et La Transfert de Mérite dans le Bouddhisme. In *Indological and Buddhist Studies,* edited by L.A. Hercus, et al. 393-414.
Canberra: Faculty of Asian Studies.

Pachow, Walter. 1951. A Comparative Study of the Prātimokṣa. In *Sino-Indian Studies* 4:1.

Pañca = *Pañcaviṁśatisāhasrikā Prajñāpāramitā.* Translated by Edward Conze as *The Large Sūtra on Perfect Wisdom.* Berkeley: University of California Press, 1975.

Pāsādika. 1982. Prolegomena to an English Translation of the Sūtrasamuccaya. In *Journal of the International Association of Buddhist Studies* 5:2:101-9.

Paul, Diana. 1979. *Women in Buddhism.* Berkeley: Asian Humanities Press.

Pederson, K. Priscilla. 1979-80. Textual Data on the Ratnakūṭa. In *Buddhist Text Information* 20:1:11, 22:5:8, 28:5:11.

——1980. Notes on the Ratnakūṭa Collection. In *Journal of the International Association of Buddhist Studies* 3:2:60-66.

Pelliot catalogue. 3 vol. Edited by Marcelle Lalou as *Inventaire des Manuscrits Tibétains de Touen-Houang (Fonds Pelliot Tibétaine).* Paris, 1939-61.

Pp = Candrakīrti, *Prasannapadā.* Edited by Louis de La Vallée Poussin. Saint Petersburg, 1903-14. Translation in part by J.W. de Jong. *Cinq Chapitres de la Prasannapadā.* Paris: Geuthner, 1949.

Pradhan, P. The First Pārājika of the Dharmaguptaka-Vinaya and the Pali Sutta-vibhaṅga. In *Visva-bharati Annals* 1:1-34.

Prajñākaramati. *Pañjikā*. In *Bodhicaryāvatāra*. Edited by P.L. Vaidya. Darbhanga: Mithila Institute, 1960.

Prebish, Charles. 1975. *Buddhist Monastic Discipline*. Pennsylavania State University Press.

——1977. (With Janice Nattier.) Mahāsaṁghika Origins: The Beginnings of Buddhist Sectarianism. In *History of Religions* 16:3.

Przyluski, Jean. 1926-28. *Le Concile de Rājagṛha*. Paris: Geuthner.

——1932. (With É. Lamotte.) Bouddhisme et Upanisad. In *BEFEO* 32.

——See also *Aśokāvadāna*.

PTS = Pali Text Society, London.

PTSD = T.W. Rhys Davids and Wm. Stede, *Pāli-English Dictionary*. London: PTS, 1921-25.

PW = Perfection of Wisdom. *PWA* = *Aṣṭa*. *PWP* = *Pañca*. *PW Rg* = *Ratnaguṇa*. *PWV* = *Vajracchedikā*.

Pye, Michael. 1978. *Skilful Means*. London: Duckworth.

R. Ratnakūṭa version of *Up*.

Ratnaguṇasaṁcaya-gāthā. Edited by Akira Yuyama. Translated by Edward Conze in *Aṣṭa*.

Rawlinson. Andrew. 1977. The Position of the *Aṣṭasāhasrikā Prajñāpāramitā* in the Development of Early Mahāyāna. In Lancaster 1977.

Reynolds, Frank E. 1976. The Many Lives of Buddha. A Study of Sacred Biography and Theravāda Buddhism. In Reynolds and Donald Capps, edited, *The Biographical Process: Studies in the History and Psychology of Religion*, 37-61. The Hague: Mouton.

Rockhill, W.W. 1884. *The Life of the Buddha from Tibetan Sources*. London: Trübner.

Ruegg, David Seyfort. 1969. *La Théorie du Tathāgatagarbha et du Gotra*. Paris: EFEO.

Rumtek. See Sde-dge.

Saṁghabhedavastu of the Mūlasarvāstivāda-vinaya. Edited by Raniero Gnoli. Serie Oriental Roma 44 (1977).

Śāntideva. *Śikṣāsamuccaya*. Edited by P.L. Vaidya. Darbhanga: Mithila Institute, 1961. Edited by Cecil Bendall. St. Pétersbourg: Imperial Academy of Sciences, 1902. Translated by Cecil Bendall and W.H.D. Rouse. London, 1922.

Sbhv = *Saṁghabhedavastu*.

Sde-dge edition of the Tibetan Sacred Canon. Reprinted Delhi: Dharmacakra/Rumtek. See also Toh.

Senart, E. 1882. *Essai sur la Légende du Buddha.* 2nd edition. Paris: Leroux.

——See also *Mv.*

Sgra sbyor bam po gnyis pa. In Sonam Angdu, edited. *Tibeto-Sanskrit Lexicographical Materials.* Leh: Basgo Tongspon, 1973.

Snar-thang edition of the Tibetan Sacred Canon. Blockprint format.

Snellgrove, David. 1957. *Buddhist Himalaya.* New York: Philosophical Library.

SS = *Śikṣāsamuccaya.* See Śāntideva.

Stein collection. Edited by Louis de La Vallée Poussin. *Catalogue of the Tibetan Manuscripts from Tun-huang in the India Office Library.* London: Oxford University Press, 1962.

Śūraṁgamasamādhi-sūtra. Translated by Étienne Lamotte. In *Mélanges Chinois et Bouddhique* (13) (1965).

Suttanipāta. Edited and translated by Lord Chalmers. Harvard Oriental Series 37 (1932).

Suv = *Suvarṇaprabhāsottama-sūtra.* Edited by Johannes Nobel. Leiden: Brill, 1944. Translated by Ř.E. Emmerick as *The Sūtra of Golden Light.* London: Luzak, 1970.

Suzuki, Daisetz Teitaro. 1930. *Studies in the Laṅkāvatāra Sūtra.* London: Routledge.

——See also *Laṅkāvatāra-sūtra.*

T = *Tables du Taishō Issaikyō.* 2nd edition, 1978. *Hōbōgirin Fascicule Annexe.*

Takasaki, Jikido. 1978. Some Problems of the Tibetan Translations from Chinese Material. In Louis Ligeti, edited, *Proceedings of the Csoma de Körös Memorial Symposium.* Budapest:Akadémiai Kiadō.

Tatz, Mark. 1977. *Rebirth: The Tibetan Game of Liberation.* New York: Doubleday.

——1978. T'ang Dynasty Influences on the Early Spread of Buddhism in Tibet. In *Tibet Journal* 3:2:1-32.

——1986. *Asaṅga's Chapter on Ethics with the Commentary of Tsong-kha-pa,* the Basic Path to Awakening: *The Complete Bodhisattva.* New York: Edwin Mellen Press.

Theragāthā. Translated by C.A.F. Rhys Davids as *Psalms of the Early Buddhists,* Vol 2. London: PTS, 1964.

Thomas, E.J. 1949. *The Life of the Buddha as Legend and History.* 3rd edition. London: Routledge.

Toh = *A Complete Catalogue of the Tibetan Sacred Canons.* 1 vol. and Index. Edited by Hakuju Ui et al. Sendai: Tohoku Imperial University, 1934.

Tsukamoto, Zenryū. 1985. 2 vol. *A History of Early Chinese Buddhism.* Translated by Leon Hurvitz. Tokyo: Kodansha.

Up, Upāya = *Upāyakauśala-sūtra.* Text data at Introduction, section 7 above.

Upāli = *Upālipariprcchā-sūtra.* Edited and translated by Pierre Python. Paris: Adrien-Maisonneuve, 1973.

Vajracchedikā-sūtra. Translated by Edward Conze. In *Buddhist Wisdom Books.* London: Allen & Unwin, 1958.

Vasumitra. *A Treatise on the Eighteen Schools.* Translated by J. Masuda. In *Asia Major* 1925.

Vātsyāyana's Kāma Sūtra. Translated by S.C. Upadhaya. Bombay: Taraporavela, 1961.

Vimalakīrtinirdeśa-sūtra. Translated by Étienne Lamotte. Bibliothèque du *Muséon* 51. English translation of the French by Sara Boin as *The Teaching of Vimalakīrti.* London: PTS, 1976.

Visuddhimagga of Buddhaghosācariya. Edited by Henry Clarke Warren, revised by Dharmanada Kosambi. Harvard Oriental Series 41 (1950). Translated by Nanamoli as *The Path of Purification.* Kandy: Buddhist Publication Society, 1975.

Vk = *Vimalakīrti.*

Vm = *Visuddhimagga.*

Wayman, Alex. 1959. Studies in Yama and Māra. In *Indo-Iranian Journal* 3:44-131.

Wiltshire, Martin G. 1980. Origins of the Paccekabuddha Concept. Doctoral dissertation, University of Lancaster.

Yuyama, Akira. 1976. *Prajñā-pāramitā-ratna-guṇa-saṁcaya-gāthā.* Cambridge University Press.

INDEX OF PROPER NAMES

Persons, Places, Schools, Titles

Text only; notes are not indexed.

INDEX OF TECHNICAL TERMS

Text only; notes are not indexed. Sanskrit equivalents are mostly reconstructions, and may not apply to all occurrences.

Abhidharama, 3, 15
Account (*paryāya*) of doctrine, 1, 51, 88
Adamantine (dhṛdha-vajra) body of a Buddha, 14, 76
Aggregate (*skandha*), 25, 29-30, 80, 84
Alms (*piṇḍa*), 2, 30-32, 39, 41, 42, 78-79
Analysis (*pratisaṁkhyā*), 39-40, 51 (*vibhāga*)
Annihilationist (*ucchedavāda*), 85
Apparitional (*aupapāduka*) form of birth, 10, 54, 58
Appreciate (*anumodana*) the merit of others, 24-25, 81
Arhat ("Worthy"), 4, 7, 24, 78, 83
Art and arts (*kalā*), 2, 36, 58, 73
Aspersions. *See* Calumny
Aspiration (*praṇidhāna, āśaya*), 7, 13-14, 24, 44-47 *passim*, 55-56, 68, 86. *See also* Resolve
Assemblies (*pariṣad*), four, 1-5 *passim*, 55, 84, 85, 88
Attachment (*saṅga*), 45. *See also* Craving; Desire; Lust; Passion
Attention, focus one's (*samanvāharati*), 28
Attraction, four means of (*catvari saṁgraha-vastūni*), 48, 52
Auditor (*śrāvaka*), 4, 10, 16, 26-30 *passim*, 46, 52, 79, 84. Stage of the 29, 30, 36, 42, 47-8, 87. Vehicle of the 29-31 *passim*, 38, 88
Austerities (*vrata*), 2, 34, 53, 62-66 *passim*
Awakening (bodhi), 1, 2, 5, 10-13 *passim*, 26-33 *passim*, 48, 51-2, 56, 59, 62-66, 73-4. Site of (*bodhimaṇḍa*; and Tree, *vṛkṣa*), 53, 57, 67-71. Aids to (*bodhi-pakṣa*), 67-8, 82. Limbs of (*bodhi-aṅga*), 84. Thought of (*bodhicitta*), 25-26, 32-33, 41-45, 49, 54, 59, 70, 82, 85, 88. *See also* Omniscience
Awareness (*samprajanya*), 66. *See also* Mindfulness
Bodhisattva, 1-16 *passim*, 23-25, 26-29, 30-31, 33-39, 41, 44-45, 48, 49, 51, 52, 53, 62-66, 73, 80-81, 84, 87-88.
Śākyamuni formerly as a, 2, 9-10, 51-71. Great hero (*Mahāsattva*), 2, 16, 23-29, 31, 38, 46-51, 53, 66-67, 69, 86-87, 96. *See also* names of Bodhisattvas in the Index of Proper Names
Body (*rūpa*), 28, 33, 36, 40-43 *passim*, 54-55, 59, 67, 72. Of a Buddha (*kāya*), 3, 9-10, 13-14, 75, 82-83
Brahman, 2, 63-66 *passim*, 78-85 *passim*. Stations of (*brahma-vihāra*), 34. Youth (*mānavaka;* and Girl, *mānavikā*), 2, 34, 51, 58, 62-65, 79-80
Buddha, 9-12 *passim*, 13, 26-27, 31-32, 42, 51, 58-59, 63-65, 87. field (*kṣetra*) of a, 33, 39. *See also* Pure Land. Stage (*bhūmi*) of a, 26, 30. *See also* Independent Buddha; Bodies of a Buddha; names of Buddhas in the Index of Proper Names
Buddhas, 10-12, 23, 25-26, 27, 43-44, 62-63, 64-65, 74, 82, 84
Buddhahood, 1, 4, 9-11 *passim*, 14, 24, 28, 37, 48. *See also* Omniscience
Calm (*śamatha*), 31, 69. *See also* Concentration; Meditation; Trance
Calumny (also, "aspersions", *apavāda*) of the Buddha, 79-90
Carelessness (*pramāda*), 38-40, 56. *See also* Vigilance
Celibacy (*brahmacarya*), 3, 5, 15-16, 30, 34, 80
Compassion (*karuṇā*), 26, 33-34, 46, 53, 56, 69, 73-74. *See also* Love; Pity
Conceit (*matta*), 54. *See also* Pride
Concentration (*samādhi*), 10-12, 25-26, 46, 52-53, 60, 67. *See also* Calm; Meditation; Trance
Confession (*deśanā*) of misdeeds, 30, 31, 33, 35, 43, 66, 76. *See also* Disclosure
Contentment (*saṁtuṣṭa*), 61, 67, 79.
Conviction that phenomena are unarising